Parents Divided,
Parents Multiplied

Parents Divided, Parents Multiplied

Margaret O. Hyde
and
Elizabeth Held Forsyth, M.D.

Westminster/John Knox Press
Louisville, Kentucky

Book design by Gene Harris

Published by Westminster/John Knox Press
Louisville, Kentucky

PRINTED IN THE UNITED STATES OF AMERICA

9 8 7 6 5 4 3 2 1

Library of Congress Cataloging-in-Publication Data

Hyde. Margaret O. (Margaret Oldroyd), date–
   Parents divided, parents multiplied / Margaret O. Hyde and
Elizabeth Held Forsyth. — 1st ed.
         p.   cm.
   Rev. ed. of: My friend has four parents / Margaret O. Hyde. c1981.
   Bibliography: p.
   Includes index.
   SUMMARY: Examines various situations that arise from divorce and
remarriage, including one-parent families, stepfamilies, and living
part-time with both parents. Also includes information on custody,
parental kidnapping, and sources of outside help.
   ISBN 0-664-32727-3

   1. Divorce—United States—Juvenile literature. 2. Remarriage—
United States—Juvenile literature. 3. Children of divorced parents—
United States—Life skills guides—Juvenile literature. [1. Divorce.
2. Remarriage. 3. Stepparents.] I. Forsyth, Elizabeth Held. II. Hyde,
Margaret O. (Margaret Oldroyd), date–   My friend has four par-
ents. III. Title.
HQ834.H93 1989
306.8'7—dc19   88-27830
                                                          CIP
                                                          AC

Contents

1

Changing Families

This is an age of changing families. Original families break apart and new ones form so often that one million children are affected each year.

For many children, the only happy families are on television. Members of these fictional families are understanding and forgiving, and the episodes always seem to end with a conclusion that satisfies everyone. Real-life families are seldom as happy as the families on TV, and they are seldom able to solve their problems as neatly and easily. No one lives in an ideal family.

Can you imagine having four parents, eight grandparents, and five stepbrothers and stepsisters? This is true for some children whose parents have been divorced and are remarried. Changing families have been given many names, such as the extended family, stepfamily, blended family, reconstituted family, and conjugal continuation. Perhaps you and some of your friends have more than two parents.

Or perhaps you live with just one parent. About

one quarter of all children now live in single-parent households, and it is predicted that 60 percent of the children born in 1989—three out of five—will spend part of their lives in one or more step relationships or as a part of a single-parent household.

Suppose you were the youngest in the family until your father remarried and his new wife brought two very small children into the household. Would you feel jealous when he picked them up and swung them around the way he used to swing you?

Blended families face unique demands and challenges in addition to those common in all families. Almost all parents and children have disagreements about things such as household responsibilities, finances, discipline, and communication between adolescents and adults. Living in a stepfamily may be especially difficult because the stepfamily has many qualities that place additional emotional burdens on its members. For example, there may be feelings of conflicting loyalties, of unexpected resentment, of disappointment with hopes that don't come true, and of not belonging. However, a National Institutes of Health–funded investigation found that stepchildren view their own mental health to be as good as that of other children. This study also found that stepchildren were as successful and as achieving as other children. On the other hand, there are studies that do not agree with these conclusions.

Living in a one-parent home can have special problems. The feelings of abandonment, sadness, guilt about being the cause of divorce, and other problems are described in this book. Children who have lost a parent through death are especially vulnerable to feelings of guilt and abandonment. They may be afraid to love again because they feel they would not be so miserable now if they had not loved the dead parent so much. Perhaps, they feel, it is better not to love at all. Some children even blame the parent who is left to carry on for the death of the missing parent.

Many people are concerned about the instability of today's families. Consider Philip, who was married to Maria for ten years. They had two young children, and then Maria became pregnant again. After the baby was born, she developed complications and died within three weeks. Four months later, Philip married Suzanne, a widow with two children, and they had two children. Suzanne died at age thirty-five, and within six months the widower married Laura. This marriage produced two more children. Because his farm was not large enough to support nine children, Philip sent the three oldest to live with their dead mother's brother, where they worked to earn their room and board. This household was composed of a complicated group: Laura, the mother of two children and stepmother to seven children of two other mothers, two of whom were not related by blood to either Laura or Philip. The family members did not get along, and they experienced much discord and tension. Today one would think they should go to a mental health professional for family therapy, but such a thing was impossible: this family lived in France about two hundred years ago.

Philip's story is not unusual. Domestic groups of the past were even less stable than the modern family. Because of the high mortality rate, a man might have a succession of wives and children from several marriages. Sometimes orphaned older children were sent to live with other relatives. A young widower tended to remarry very soon after the death of his wife, as it was necessary for him to have someone to care for his small children, attend to the household, and help with the farm chores. In one region of France, according to records from the seventeenth and eighteenth centuries, most remarriages occurred within six months of the death of the first wife.

In some areas, such as in mountain regions, the father had to seek seasonal work, which meant moving away from home temporarily. His wife became a single parent, shouldering all the responsibilities of the farm and the family. Sometimes the husband did not send money home, and occasionally he stayed away permanently. When this occurred, the woman might then take another man into the house to live with her. This is another situation that is familiar in the present as well as the past.

The mixed families of today are mainly the result of divorce and remarriage, not death or desertion, but the effects on the children are probably not very different from the effects of multiple marriages in former times. No one really knows what the psychological impact was, but you can see that people in former times faced some of the same problems that we confront now.

Even though each family situation is unique, many problems are common to children who live in families with other than their two biological parents. The examples in the following pages may help you and your friends to live more comfortably with parents divided and multiplied. Some of the ways of working through problems may be useful to you and to your friends who are challenged by such problems.

No matter how many people are part of your family and no matter how they are related to you, your family is still the place to go when you feel the need for intimacy. The family is the source of emotional support for its members even though the members may be changing. The traditional relationships that evolve slowly in the original family may never be replaced when parents divorce and remarry, but the new family can still provide some of its basic functions, such as shelter, food, and loving care. While many people claim that divorce is destroying the family, some experts remind us that divorce is not rejection of the family but of a spouse. The family, although smaller or larger, remains.

Adjusting to a changing family can be very difficult. Sometimes it is comforting just to know that other people have lived through situations that are similar to or worse than yours or your friends'. Most of all, it is good to know that tomorrow can be brighter.

2

Coming Unglued

"The only thing worse than divorce is death," Grammy remarked the day after Mike's parents told him they were going to separate. On that day, Mike, who was an only child, agreed with her.

Mike's family had been sitting around the kitchen table the night before. His parents had seemed preoccupied during supper, and after the dishes had been cleared away, his father announced that he was leaving that night. He and Mike's mother were going to live in different houses from now on. Mike's father said that he and Mom had not been getting along well for some time. Mike knew this to be true, for his parents constantly quarreled. Mike had grown to take this for granted.

Mike held himself very still. Even the kitchen seemed strangely quiet as his father explained that everyone argues from time to time, but he and Mom disagreed almost every time they spoke to each other. They irritated each other so much that they both decided it was time to separate. It was time for a divorce.

Mike felt like crying, but he held back the tears. He didn't say anything at all because there were too many things he wanted to ask all at once. What was going to happen to him? Where would he live? What had he done to cause the separation?

Mike squirmed in his chair while his mother spoke to him about the problems she and Dad were having. She explained that they had made many mistakes during their marriage and now their mistakes were beyond repair. She said she was sorry she had been cross to Mike at times when she felt unhappy. Some of the times she had been cross to Mike she had really been upset with Dad.

While his mother and father continued to talk to him, Mike wondered what he would tell his friends. What would they say? Some of them had parents who no longer lived together. Some of them seemed to manage living with mothers part of the time and with fathers part of the time. Mike had always thought this could never happen in his family.

Finally, Mike asked, "What will happen to me?"

"You will live with me, Mike," his mother told him. "I've seen a smaller house I like. It will be more convenient for both of us. As soon as we get things cleared up here, we'll move there. Your dad is taking a job in another city. It's about a thousand miles away from here."

"I'll still love you, Mike," his father assured him. "I will always love you and help to take care of you."

Mike wondered how his father could take care of him when he was so far away, but he didn't say anything. He was more concerned now about where he and his mother would live. He felt somewhat better when he learned that the new house would be in the same school district. Joe, a new boy in his class, had moved from another part of the country because his parents had separated. Joe still seemed very lost. Mike thought he would make a special effort to be nice to him when he saw him tomorrow.

Then Mike asked to be excused. He left the table quietly and went to watch television. The television set was in the next room and even when Mike turned it on, he could hear his parents telling each other that things went well and that he did not seem very upset. Somehow he couldn't show them how awful he felt. He loved both his mother and his father and wanted to be with them both. He tried to think of how he could persuade them to get together again, but he felt frozen inside.

As the days went by and Mike thought more and more about the divorce plans, he grew certain that he was responsible. Mike had heard his father say several times that he could not live in the house any longer, and Mike remembered things he had done each time that had upset his father. For example, he remembered his father saying this the day after Mike had broken the glass top of the coffee table. Another time his father stayed out all night after Mike had spilled a box of cereal all over the kitchen floor. Mike did not realize that his father had barely noticed these things. He had no way of knowing that his father was too busy with his own problems.

It was many weeks before Mike's feelings improved enough that he could disagree with Grammy's statement that the only thing worse than divorce is death. He had a new friend in Joe, who listened to his problems and pointed out that there were even some new things that were good. For one thing, the house was very peaceful without his parents' constant quarreling.

Feeling Guilty

Many young people think they are the cause of their parents' divorce, as Mike did. This is especially true around the time of separation. They associate their own behavior with their parents' problems even though the children may have had nothing at all to do with them.

Many children express their feeling of guilt in the following ways: "My allowance was too big. If I don't take any allowance for the next year, you will not have to fight over money." "I'll stop quarreling with my sister. Then you will be happier and Dad will not have to leave." "I promise not to be bad anymore."

Why do so many young people blame themselves? Psychiatrists believe that the child's feeling of guilt about the separation involves a notion of control even though this notion is not realized. A child feels helpless about changing his parents' minds to go ahead with a divorce, but if the child was the cause of their decision to separate, perhaps he or she can do something to reverse the decision.

For example, Kim felt very guilty about the trouble she had caused by staying out beyond the time her parents set for her to come home. She had caused many arguments about this, she knew, and she had even convinced her mother that her father was being overly strict. When Kim learned of her parents' plans for divorce, she promised to obey her father's rules for being home on time. She even offered to come home earlier than the time he set.

Kim was so distressed she discussed her guilty feelings with her counselor at school, even though she did not enjoy talking about her family with strangers. The counselor explained to her that there were some things she could change and some things over which she had no control. He told Kim that her hopes of preventing her parents from separating with better behavior were not realistic. He stressed that Kim must resign herself to the reality that she was not the cause of the problem. What Kim had done in the past had not caused the divorce plans, and what she did in the future would not change them. The counselor helped Kim see some things she could do to lessen the pain of separation. When Kim recognized this, she stopped feeling guilty.

Many counselors and therapists help young people who feel responsible for their parents' separation by explaining the unconscious desire for control. They help young people to see the dynamics of divorce, looking at it through the eyes of parents rather than through their own eyes. They point out that children are not usually the cause of problems in a husband-wife relationship, and they help the boys and girls understand that parents divorce each other, not their children. When children recognize that it is not within their power to control certain things, such as divorce, the feeling of being responsible is lifted. Then they can proceed to do the things they *can* control, such as developing positive things in their lives. For example, they can involve themselves in more meaningful relationships with other children and adults to try to make up for the partial or total absence of a parent.

Even though parents reassure a child that the decision to divorce rests entirely on their own problems and the child is in no way at fault, children do not usually believe them. In a group of thirty junior high school students of divorced parents who met weekly, twenty-eight expressed the belief that they were to blame for their parents' divorce. At first, many blamed one parent, then the other, but eventually they blamed themselves. In most cases, the blaming was silent and would not have been expressed except for the group discussion in which the counselor asked a direct question about blame. Privately, they had been telling themselves time after time, "I'm hopeless. If I had been better, Mom would not have started to drown her troubles in drink. I can't do anything right. I'd better stop making mistakes, or I'll cause trouble for other people the way I did for my mother and father."

Unfortunately, silently accepting the blame for a divorce can interfere with a person's feelings throughout a lifetime. This blame can lower self-esteem, a quality on which much growth depends. Of course, a child's actions *may* play a major part in causing a divorce, but this is seldom the case. Most children who feel guilty see their part as greater than it really is.

Feeling Lost

Many kinds of feelings can get mixed up when family members separate. One very common feeling among children of divorced parents is that of abandonment. One very young child lived with his father after his mother left the family. They walked in the park together every afternoon. Whenever the child saw a woman who looked slightly like his mother coming toward him, he would run ahead of his father, throw himself at the woman, and cling to her until he could be convinced that she was not his mother. One time after he accepted that the woman he was hugging was not really his mother, the boy cried openly. Then he clung to his father and begged his father not to leave him.

Feeling abandoned and concerned that the remaining parent will leave is a common experience for many children of divorce. Consider the case of seven-year-old Martha, whose mother and father often told her how awful the other one was. Martha's father complained he was ignored by his family. No one was interested in his work or his guitar playing—a hobby that absorbed most of his time. Her mother felt neglected, too, and claimed that the father had no time for his family. After they separated, Martha's mother announced that her father had deserted them for the woman who lived down the street. Actually, the father did leave quietly one night without saying goodbye to Martha or giving her any assurance that he would ever see her again.

Martha slept poorly after her father left home. She called her mother often during the night and said she heard noises that might be her father coming back to his room. Although the mother explained that he would never come back to live with them, she tried to comfort the little girl and told Martha that she might be able to visit him in his new home. But the restless nights continued. And some nights Martha thought she heard her mother packing her bags. She feared that her mother might slip away as her father had. Martha's fears developed into nightmares of being abandoned, which stopped only when she saw a therapist who helped her to understand and believe that her mother would not abandon her, too.

Then there is Eric. Eric tried very hard to be good. He had been told that his mother had sent his "bad" father away, and he did not want this to happen to him. His good behavior made his mother very happy until she began to realize that something was wrong. Eric seemed always on guard and too eager to please. His mother began to wonder if Eric really meant what he said or if he was telling her what he thought she wanted to hear. Actually, this made Eric's mother angry with him because he was not being frank with her. By trying to be good he was not himself, and this made him uncomfortable. Eric and his mother discussed the problem, and Eric felt better when his mother assured him that she would not send him away no matter what he did.

Even when a parent can't visit a child because he or she lives too far away, some children of divorced parents interpret the loss as abandonment. There are cases where boys and girls are so afraid of being abandoned by the remaining parent that they use a variety of maneuvers to deny their fear and sadness: they play with matches, they run heedlessly across streets in front of traffic, and they climb in dangerous places. Psychiatrists sometimes attribute these actions to children's attempts to prove they cannot be harmed. This kind of behavior is sometimes a bid for attention, which is meant to make the parent stay close by to watch and protect the child. Many children are helped only by the knowledge that the parent who left the family abandoned his or her spouse, not the child.

Some children see their parents' behavior at the time of a family's breaking apart as childish and lose their sense of trust in them. The children feel unprotected because their parents seem unable to care even for themselves. Sometimes remarks made by one parent about the other parent's worthlessness cause the child to feel concerned or lost. But as time goes on children grow to realize that this was a time of crisis when many remarks were exaggerated. There is comfort for some in knowing that even if both parents were to abandon them, a situation that is unlikely to happen, grandparents or other adults would care for them.

Parents who do not have custody of their children express their interest in different degrees. They vary on the one extreme from those who consider the child first in their lives to those who break completely with their offspring. Both extremes may be harmful, depending on the particular situation, but the parent who completely ignores a child may be the more difficult for a child to understand. Sometimes, the remaining parent makes excuses for the neglectful one, to protect the child from feelings of abandonment. The mother may make remarks such as "Your father really loves you. He just does not know how to show his love." Or, if a birthday is forgotten, the father may say, "Your mother never did have a very good memory." Young children see their parents as infallible, and therefore it is traumatic for them to realize that a parent has failed in any way and to recognize that both parents cannot be right.

Fortunately, there are very few parents who cut themselves off completely from their children. In some cases, the problem is complicated. Some may try to make a complete break with the other parent in spite of the harm to the child. The custodial parent may try to make a complete break with the absent parent, thinking that this may be the best for the child. And some may cut off contact with the other parent for selfish reasons, ignoring their child's needs.

In Paul's case, it was the mother who was selfish. Ten-year-old Paul was the oldest of three children. He had responded to his father's departure by curling up in a closet and sobbing for long periods of time. Now and then, he would telephone his father and beg him to return. Paul was very frightened about the future and felt torn in two. As time passed, Paul came to side entirely with his mother, who continued to attack the father verbally. For example, the mother told the children that they would have to give up their dog because their father was not providing enough money for dog food. Actually, he was supplying a large amount of support money, but they had no way of knowing that their father had not abandoned them.

Several months after Paul's initial response to the separation (in which he hid in the closet), Paul stopped pleading with his father to return. He helped his mother to turn his sisters against the father and rejected his father's attempts to see the family. He even returned his gifts.

All the children in this family felt abandoned by their father, even though he really was trying desperately to have a good relationship with them. The mother was working out her anger at her ex-husband by using the children. In cases such as this, a parent may just give up trying to see the children, even though the desire is there. The deceit of one parent hurts and confuses the rest of the family.

Many therapists feel there is something seriously wrong with a person who does not express love for a child. Mary was an unusually mature girl who was able to understand this. She could appreciate the fact that just because her father did not show love for her did not mean that she was unlovable. Friends and other adults love her now and many will do so in the future. The defect is with her parent, not with her. Unfortunately, this is very difficult, if not impossible, for most children to understand. Children in this situation may well be angry at the neglectful parent. Many feel depressed. It is more appropriate to have a feeling of pity for the person who is missing the rich experience of loving and rearing one's own child, but a child would find this very difficult to believe under these circumstances.

Some degree of rejection by a parent is not the same as total abandonment. There may be times that a parent who wishes to be with a child finds inconvenient or actually impossible. This does not mean that the parent does not love the child. In all human relationships, there are complications and mood swings. Just because a parent grows angry with a child or is bored with a relationship from time to time, or even several times in one day, does not mean that the parent does not love the child. Many parents have problems that take a great deal of their time and make them irritable or prevent the free expression of love. They do not explain this to their children, and therefore the children draw the wrong conclusion from their actions. They think their parents don't love them.

Only a small percentage of fathers and mothers really do not love their children. These adults have many good qualities but are deficient in their ability to love. Such parents do not enjoy doing things with their children. They do not want to hold them or touch them, even for a second or two. They do not show pride in their children or in their children's accomplishments, and they really do not want to spend time with them. If you think your parent does not love you, it may only seem that way. You may need to talk this over with an adult counselor who is trained to look at the situation from all sides.

Some boys and girls try many things to get a parent to show interest in them. Acting naughty or too good are ways of gaining attention, for example. Many children find it difficult to accept the fact that a parent is not perfect, and some refuse to do so. They make idols of the absent parent, using all kinds of excuses for the neglect. Many of these children are happier if they are helped by Scout leaders, Big Brothers or Big Sisters, or leaders in some of the organizations mentioned in the list at the back of the book.

Feeling Sad

Divorce makes most children sad at first. Many go through a period of mourning that is not as intense as when a parent dies but that follows the same stages. At first, they find it impossible to believe that their family has come unglued. Then they become sad because they do not see one parent as often as before, and memories of the missing person fill the mind. Crying is a good way to express this sadness. Angry feelings and guilty feelings follow, although many of these stages overlap. Grief is a process by which one reaches a stage of healthy detachment from the past that makes it possible to reach out for new experiences. Even though sadness at the loss of the original family may never leave completely, it need not keep one from having a happy and full life.

Jim felt very depressed for several weeks after his father left. Then he began to become involved with helping set up the new living arrangements. Even though he grumbled about doing some of the household chores, it made him feel better to be responsible for the same unpleasant everyday tasks that he had always done. Certainly, much in his life had changed. Like almost all children who experience the divorce of parents, he wished that the family would reunite. Jim wanted his father to come back, and he wished all aspects of his life would return to normal. Even though his mother and father had argued much of the time, he wanted the days to be the way they used to be. He found there was a certain amount of comfort for him in the familiar. But like most human beings, Jim was resilient. After a few weeks, he accepted his sadness at the loss of his father's day-to-day presence and began to make a new life for himself.

In certain cases, the time after divorce can be better in some ways than the time when parents were arguing, or when an alcoholic parent caused problems for the family, or when some other very difficult situation existed. Although children are sad and miss the absent parent, there is a sense of relief in having a more peaceful home.

Even the young people who find life terribly sad immediately after parents separate discover that they can get used to living in a single-parent household or a new situation. The painful feelings hurt less and less. There are even cases where boys and girls see more of their fathers after a divorce than they did when the family was supposedly intact. In any case, feelings of sadness and helplessness won't last forever.

Feeling Angry

Boys and girls of all ages are angry about the divorce of their parents, and to some degree feelings of anger at such a time are reasonable. Adolescents may be especially angry because they feel that their parents' separation has increased their problems at an especially difficult time in their lives. Some condemn both parents for the way they have acted, while others are angry with just one parent. Imagine how you would feel if you could no longer respect the parent you have especially admired and identified with. You would feel angry and disappointed because you could no longer look to that parent as a guide.

It is often difficult to recognize the anger that comes at separation, but expressing anger, talking about it, and exploring the reasons for it helps to resolve these feelings. Denying anger can make things worse. Repressing anger may mean that it is channeled into neurotic behavior. One boy became very conscious of his nose after his father left home. Not only did he spend a great deal of time thinking about his nose and looking at it in the mirror, he noticed other people's noses and compared them to his own. He had no idea that this obsession with noses was at all related to his feelings of guilt and hostility at losing his father until a doctor helped him work out his problems.

When the causes of anger are not recognized, the hostility felt by children of divorced parents can be expressed in an unlimited number of ways. For example, a boy may equate antisocial behavior with masculinity, a view encouraged by many television programs. Since he is living with a female parent, he may fear that some of her femininity may rub off on him and make him unmanly. He may also identify with the absent male parent through attempts to prove his masculinity. He will choose friends who belong to a tough gang that considers shoplifting, vandalism, and other antisocial behavior a mark of masculinity, unaware that this is his way of expressing anger and gaining a false sense of power.

Mark, on the other hand, was a boy who had already expressed his anger directly so there was no need for acting angry when he was asked to join a gang of boys who were heavily involved with drugs. He considered joining them, but he felt secure in spite of the fact that his parents were divorced. He knew they both loved him, even though they no longer loved each other. When one of the boys called him chicken for not trying a capsule of unknown contents, Mark was comfortable about refusing. He even told them that taking such a capsule was a stupid thing to do, not brave or daring.

Some children engage in destructive acts to try to gain the attention of a parent, such as running into traffic, dieting excessively, or engaging in other hazardous activities. They may unconsciously feel that punishment is better than no attention at all, but later they find that this further alienates the parent for whom they are reaching. Acting out or other undesirable behavior may also be an expression of depression by children who suffer from sadness rather than anger.

Instant Adult

Twelve-year-old Sue was an only child, and she was expected to act like an adult. Both her mother and father were very ambitious about getting ahead. They expected Sue to excel in everything she did. Sue's father had traveled a great deal for many years, and her mother spent every day doing volunteer work at the local hospital. Sue's mother grew more and more involved with the hospital programs and was delighted when she was invited to join the trustees, most of whom were men. There were many night meetings, so Sue had to take over many of the family chores that would normally have been done by her mother. She was able to manage this well until her father stopped traveling and she was put in the role of homemaker for her father. Sue was upset by this, but her mother would not give up her volunteer activities. When Sue's mother became interested in one of the doctors at the hospital and moved out of the house, both parents agreed to a divorce. Sue was left at home to care for her father. He seemed jealous of her friends and talked with her much as he would talk to someone his own age. Sue felt the heavy burden of his problems. She even thought about running away. Instead, she found help in talking with the counselor at school, who persuaded her father to discuss his problems with a psychiatrist or psychologist.

Many parents use their children as a substitute for the missing spouse. Ralph was glad that his mother did not expect him to be the man of the house after her divorce. She made it clear that he was not expected to "make up for Daddy now that he is away." She would still make the big decisions, although she promised to discuss some things with him. Ralph was glad he did not have to listen to the people who told him, "Now that your father is gone, you will have to take care of your mother."

Today Is Not Forever

Feelings of sadness, hurt, anger, and anxiety are common at the time a family is coming unglued. Although people handle these feelings in different ways, it is good to know that it is healthy to express some of these emotions by discussing them. Children and parents are distressed by divorce, but the distress lessens with time. Bit by bit, most children and parents find they have not lost their happy selves forever. Just knowing this can help.

3

Living
with One Parent

The Father-Son Dinner notices were fun for everyone in the class but Tim. His father lived far away and Tim never saw him except during holidays, when Tim was shipped off for a visit. Tim's teacher suggested that he bring an uncle or a friend of the family to the dinner. Tim had done this last year, shortly after his parents were divorced, and he had had a good time, but it was not the same. He really missed his father. Now that the intense pain and suffering of the period immediately following the separation had disappeared, Tim had a sad, resigned attitude about the divorce. Most of the time he did not think much about the loss of his father in everyday family life. It was just on occasions like the Father-Son Dinner when the whole bad scene came back to him.

Tim was not the only one in his class who did not live with his father. One of the girls never knew her father; her mother had never married. Another boy saw his father on weekends and lived with his mother during the week. Since this boy's father lived nearby, he would come to the dinner. One boy had a stepfather who had been around ever since he could remember. He had no problem about asking him to the Father-Son Dinner.

Some children find living with a single parent very difficult, while others get along as well or even better than some of the children who live with two parents. This is especially true when the parents do not get along well.

Single-Parent Homes Can Be Secure

There are many studies about the impact of divorce on children. Most show that the separation of parents is an acutely painful experience for children. Still, they indicate that one stable and well-functioning parent within a home can make a child feel secure and grow normally. When problems between parent and child persist, it is quite possible that some of the trouble may have been there before the divorce or might have developed anyway. Some authorities even see divorce as a challenge. With enough support from parents, children learn to develop their own resources and gain a sense of mastery while doing so.

Consider the problem of twelve-year-old Jean, who was never allowed to make decisions for herself. Every time her friends asked her to go to the corner store with them, Jean had to ask her mother. Her mother decided what clothes she should wear each day, planned her activities, chose her playmates, and did most of Jean's thinking for her. Jean was more protected than ever after her parents separated. Her mother had no interests in life other than Jean, and she really felt she was being a good mother by devoting all her time to her daughter. Unfortunately, when Jean became an adolescent, she rebelled against authority and ran away from home. She was exposed to young people who introduced her to drugs and prostitution. Both she and her mother encountered crisis situations for which they were ill prepared.

Rachel, on the other hand, grew up in a family where she was encouraged to make her own decisions. Although her parents were strict about setting limits, they encouraged Rachel to solve problems by using her own resources whenever the opportunity arose. After her parents separated, Rachel was better able to deal with the emotional problems that all children of divorce encounter to some degree. Her self-confidence helped her to meet the crisis of losing contact with her father and to make a good home life with her mother that was free of the constant arguing that had been part of her life before.

Each person's situation differs a great deal and the cases of Jean and Rachel are two extremes. Each parent and each child is unique, but some patterns can be recognized and changed before serious problems develop. For example, if the anger, sadness, feelings of abandonment, and other early reactions to separation have not begun to fade by the end of a year and a young person living with a

single parent is still miserable, the help of a counsel-
or may be needed.

Life for Mother

Many young people who live with one parent are
aware of the special problems that a mother or father
alone may have. Divorce is a very painful experience
for parents too. Many times, a single parent com-
bines long hours of earning a living with the day-to-
day problems of parenting. When single-parent families have been part of a two-parent family at some
time but have lost one parent because of death or
divorce, the social life of the remaining parent
changes. Many single parents suffer from fear,
loneliness, isolation, guilt, failure, and other negative
emotions. Their children bury their fears and become
more insecure.

Just as children must make many adjustments
after separation, parents too have to learn to live in a
different kind of world. For some it is better, for some
it is worse. For all, it is a time of change.

Mrs. Singer was very lonely after her divorce. She
thought most of her friends sided with her husband.
(Actually, they decided to ignore the Singers so they
would not be accused of taking sides.) Mrs. Singer
tried to make new friends so that she would not have
to depend entirely on the children for companionship. First, she joined a woman's club, but she found
that most of the members were cool to her. Even
though she volunteered to help with some of the
activities, she did not feel that she had much in
common with a group of women whose families

were still intact. Besides, the schedule conflicted with her part-time job as a waitress. Since she had never worked outside the home before, she found the job especially exhausting.

However, Mrs. Singer continued to reach out to other adults. She thought she might make new friends by taking an evening course at the local high school. She did discover that the people in her class were friendly before and after class, but no one really seemed interested in spending any time with her outside the classroom. The next semester, she took a course that offered field trips to study historic buildings in the area. Here she had a better chance to chat with people. One member of the class was a woman whose husband had just left her, and she was glad to meet someone like Mrs. Singer who would join new groups with her. As her life grew more interesting, Mrs. Singer became more relaxed at home and was able to deal with her children's problems more easily. She even found it helpful to discuss her decisions about them with several members of a group who ran a thrift shop for the hospital. This helped her to set limits and enforce rules that made family life run more smoothly.

In the single-parent family, only one parent is responsible for rules. While this can seem over-whelming to the parent, it may make life simpler for a child. Certainly, Ellen's life was more comfortable. Before her parents were divorced, Ellen's mother kept one set of rules and her father insisted on another. Ellen knew she could start an argument any time she wanted by telling her father that she did not have to be home at the time he set because her mother said this time was unreasonable. With one less opinion to be reckoned with, there was more stability in the home.

Many single parents feel overwhelmed by the responsibilities that come with tending to children's needs, earning money, paying bills, and handling all the everyday matters that were once shared by two people. Some discover that they have little time for themselves, and this makes them depressed. Since depression drains energy from an individual, the situation grows worse. Children who are old enough to understand that a parent needs some time and energy for personal pleasures can help by taking some of the responsibility for running the house. They may discover that this participation helps make life better for them, too.

The Good with the Bad

According to some experts, the children in a single-parent home may have an advantage because their help is needed in doing household chores. In a two-parent house, there may be nothing left for a child to do other than watch television or play. There is no participation with other members of the family in washing cars, doing housework, cooking meals, and so on. Understanding this point of view may be very difficult for the people doing the chores, but there is real value in working with other members of the family.

Another interesting advantage has been observed for some college students who come from single-parent homes. A number of studies suggest that children who share management with their mothers in single-parent homes exhibit greater verbal skills than children in two-parent homes. Perhaps this is due to their closeness to the mother. For example, a study of men who were entering Stanford University showed that students who lived in single-parent homes with their mothers for at least one year in their childhood scored higher than other students in the language part of aptitude tests. The scores were no lower in mathematical sections. This may or may not be true for those who spent time in a single-parent home in which the father was the only parent.

Many experts are finding that divorce may offer some benefits for both parents and children after the initial difficult times pass. Like two-parent homes, single-parent homes can be happy or unhappy. Although there may be many periods of confusion and conflict, it is possible to come through the experience with few scars and to turn the challenges into periods of growth.

Life for Father

While most children who live with a single parent live with their mother, more and more are spending most of their time with a father. Nine out of ten children of divorce in the past were assigned to the care of their mothers with or without visitation rights for the father. The father was considered as the one to care for the children most of the time only if the mother was considered unfit for moral reasons or on account of some emotional or physical handicap. Today, some mothers are choosing careers in which the full-time care of children interferes, and they are relieved to have the children live with their father. And many fathers seem glad to take advantage of the trend for men to exhibit more nurturing qualities. They feel quite capable and successful in their ability to be the primary parent for their children, even though not many of these fathers grew up in families where they learned to mend, clean house, cook, and do other household chores. Along with working mothers, single fathers enlist the help of their older children and lean on groups such as Big Sisters, Big Brothers, and Foster Grandparents for support. Their pride in being able to cope with the challenge of parenthood and watch their children mature under their guidance usually makes up for the problems caused by their inexperience in running a house and the many adjustments they must make.

Two Parents in One?

Some parents tend to overcompensate for the absent parent by trying to be both mother and father to their children. There is more concern about boys than girls. Some believe a fatherless boy may be less aggressive or more effeminate than one raised by both parents, and that later in life he may have difficulty in his role as a husband and father. Even though a parent of the same sex serves as a role model for the child's own sex role, however, there has been no evidence to suggest that it is necessary to have a father in the home in order for boys to learn the nature of the roles, responsibilities, and behaviors considered appropriate to men. Just as children whose parents speak no English soon learn to speak the language fluently from people outside the home, older brothers, older boys in the neighborhood, Big Brothers, uncles, or neighbors can serve as role models for the traditional masculine traits. It may be comforting for boys in a fatherless home to know that the images on television of boys and their fathers spending a lot of time fishing, building models, and playing touch football do not often reflect real life.

According to some experts, fathers in middle- and lower-income families spend only about twenty-five minutes each week in direct one-to-one contact with their sons. The single mother's attitude toward men and the degree to which she allows her boy freedom to develop his own identity seem to be the keys to his development in a fatherless home. This whole subject of the importance of masculine traits versus feminine traits is one of controversy in today's world, but many psychiatrists, psychologists, and other experts still feel that it is important for boys and girls to have a role model of the same sex.

Some experts believe that girls living with their mothers as head of the household show a special craving for male attention, but it has been shown that boys who live in fatherless families also crave male attention. This may be due to a need for all young children of divorce to regain a father figure. One might expect to find a special craving for women when children live with a father as the only parent.

The presence of role models does appear to help children with sex identification, as do positive comments about people of a child's own sex from the parent of the opposite sex. The most important years for sex identification come between the ages of thirty months and five years and at early adolescence. Perhaps you can help by acting as a role model for a sister or young person in your neighborhood who lives in a single-parent family.

Parents Without Partners

No matter whether a single parent is a mother or a father, the most important source of security for boys and girls is a competent, self-confident parent. Many single-parent families find practical solutions to some of their problems through organizations such as Parents Without Partners. This organization began on a hot summer day at a beach back in 1956 when two divorced people were discussing how different their lives had become from what they had been and from the lives of their married friends. They wondered if getting together with other single parents might be a helpful learning experience for everyone involved. The next spring, these people placed some ads in newspapers inviting any parents without partners to a meeting where they could talk over common problems, develop a fuller life for themselves and their children, and hold discussions with psychologists and lawyers. The first meeting was held in a room provided by a church in New York City. In thirty years, the organization grew from this small beginning to become an international one with about 170,000 members and 800 local groups. There are members in all fifty states and most of the

Canadian provinces. People in many countries have used the Parents Without Partners as a model to form similar groups. The majority of the members of Parents Without Partners are single through separation or divorce, and the rest are either widowed, natural parents who never married, or single adoptive parents.

Many adults join local chapters of Parents Without Partners because their children urge them to do so. Many young people learn about the family activities they offer from other boys and girls in the classes. For example, one is a car clinic run by fathers who are mechanics and interested in young people. Chapters may have community-service programs, puppetry, creative-writing classes, softball games, and other sports, or any of about two hundred different activities. All chapters have some programs. In addition to meeting people who live in single-parent families in these activities, parents and children share in many valuable experiences through them.

Besides the family activities and the sharing of ideas between parents at adult meetings, some areas have formed chapters known as the International Youth Council. These chapters are open to adolescents between the ages of twelve and seventeen whose parents are separated, divorced, widowed, or never married. Although many of the parents are members of Parents Without Partners, this is not required for a young person to join. Advisers help with educational, recreational, and community-service programs. Panel discussions may include getting along with parents, discipline problems, disc jockeys, allowances, drugs, part-time jobs, and many other subjects. One International Youth Council chapter planned an outing they called "Night Owl Bus Ride" on which they visited police stations, hospitals, and night court. Then they had breakfast at dawn at a favorite eating place. Another chapter raised funds so they could take a week's canoe trip. Another provided a program of entertainment and games for a children's institution. Many such programs help members to develop independence, responsibility, and leadership.

Single-Parent Family Centers

Many small organizations have sprung up throughout the United States to answer various needs of single-parent families. For example, at some Young Men's and Young Women's Christian Associations (YM-YWCAs) and at some Young Men's and Young Women's Hebrew Associations (YM-YWHAs) special groups for parents and for children help them explore their feelings about divorce and the problems of living in a single-parent family. Some groups have clothing swaps, food co-ops, baby-sitting pools, joint vacations, and pot-luck suppers. The last are especially welcomed by families who find that the dinner hour is difficult because the absent parent is missed, especially at the table. The traditional family meal that was formerly a happy time is often lonely. Late evening is another difficult period, and many single parents find comfort on hotlines that are run by single-parent volunteers. Advice on how to get a job, find a lawyer, or obtain welfare benefits and housing, or just the sound of another adult voice, helps the callers. Many community-service organizations and neighborhood associations organize hotlines for single parents and for people with a variety of problems.

Schools are becoming more aware of the needs of children who live in one-parent families. In some cases, the school tries to fill some of the empty space left by the absent parent, but this is unusual. Few school budgets allow for this kind of parent-teacher interaction. Many single parents who have young children find that day-care centers provide the warmth of a missing parent until they finish work. Day-care personnel know that a child who needs loving can't be asked to wait until Mother comes home at 6 P.M. But time is needed to compensate. Many mothers with tight schedules make sure to allow for a time devoted entirely to their children. For example, one mother set aside two hours every evening for her three-year-old daughter and let nothing interfere with that time. The hours between 6 and 8 P.M. belonged to the two of them and were very special hours for both.

From Broken Homes to Family Units

Being a child or teenager in a single-parent home might have seemed unusual twenty years ago, but the stigma that went with the old name "broken home" has disappeared in many areas of the country. Classmates are often in similar situations today, and it is more common to find teachers who understand the unique and special needs of single-parent families from their own personal experiences. Today, it is realized that, with special effort, a single-parent home can provide the same security, warmth, and psychological nourishment for the healthy development of children as a two-parent home can.

4

Custody and Parental Kidnapping

"What will happen to me?" is one of the first questions children ask when hearing of their parents' plan to separate. Parents who decide where their children will live before they tell them about the divorce can readily answer the question. For some families, however, custody is a serious and continuing problem.

When ten-year-old Bobby was asked to draw a picture of how he felt about his family after a two-year custody battle, he drew a boy hanging on a tightrope that was stretched over a deep valley. A parent stood atop the mountains on either side, holding the ends of the rope. When asked what his parents were saying, Bobby told the counselor that both mother and father were trying to bribe him with promises of things he wanted. Bobby was hanging precariously in the picture; it seemed to express the fear that he might fall into the valley and be destroyed.

Another child who was asked to draw a picture of

her family at the time of a custody battle drew her mother and her brother with her but did not show her father. When asked what her father looked like, she replied, "A greedy ape."

Fortunately, most custody agreements are worked out for "the best interests of the child" without long years of legal hassles, but not everyone agrees about what is best. Certainly, the best arrangement for one family may not be the best for another family.

Types of Living Arrangements

In the most common type of custody, children live with one parent and spend some time with the other. The arrangement is specified in the divorce decree. Until the early part of this century, children were generally assigned to the care of the father, because he was considered the head of the household. Then, as the role of women in child rearing was increasingly recognized, the courts assumed that the best interests of the child were served by placing him or her with the mother.

Although mothers still get sole custody in the majority of cases, there is a trend toward joint custody. This arrangement, known as shared custody or divided custody, is one in which parents share equal responsibility in caring for the children. Those who believe in joint custody claim that prejudice in favor of mothers is based on outdated sex roles. Many fathers are not as poor at nurturing as they were once thought to be. In fact, many fathers are as good or better than their ex-wives. One reason for favoring mothers in placing children with one parent in the past was the fact that most women stayed at home. This is no longer true.

In some areas of the United States fathers have joined together in groups such as Equal Rights for Fathers and Fathers for Equal Justice to work toward bringing about changes in the routine assignment of children to their mothers. Thirty-three states have enacted legislation permitting courts to order joint custody. Parents can arrange joint custody privately in the remaining states, but it cannot be part of a court order.

Joint custody is growing in popularity in some areas. According to a survey in northern California, nearly 20 percent of the custody arrangements there were joint, while in Virginia only about 5 percent of divorces ended with joint custody.

Whether or not you consider the trend toward joint custody a good one depends on which expert you follow. According to David Levy, who is executive director of the National Council for Children's Rights, children's needs for the security and role models of mother and father are best served by joint custody. Nick Stinnett, co-author of *Secrets of Strong Families,* suggests that joint custody encourages commitment, time together, and spiritual wellness. However, a new study conducted by the Center for the Family in Transition found that joint custody arrangements do not necessarily benefit children and, in cases of bitter divorce, can be detrimental. This California study was based on only the first two years after divorce, so the researchers suggest that their conclusions be assessed cautiously.

Split custody is different from joint custody, although it amounts to sole custody as far as individual children are concerned. In this arrangement siblings are divided between the two parents. Usually the boys live with the father and the girls with the mother, but not always. As with other arrangements, the individual situation has to be considered. Some psychiatrists feel that, in general, split custody is not a good arrangement. There may be a double trauma: having to cope with the divorce *and* the loss of siblings. Brothers and sisters can be very supportive of each other in times of crisis or when parents are absent.

In all cases, parents and judges are supposed to work toward the best interests of the child even if the child does not think, at the time, that the arrangement is the best one. There is general agreement that children over the age of twelve should be consulted about custody but the final decision about what is best should be left to adults. Young children are not mature enough to know which parent can and will make the best home for them. Besides, asking a child to choose one parent over the other may provoke anxiety and guilt about loyalty. It is a no-win situation. The requests of adolescents are usually considered more seriously than those of young children. Even then, choices may be made for superficial reasons such as the promise of a private telephone.

The best arrangements are flexible enough to change as people change. This works best when parents remain friendly.

Visits with Father

Mary's home life was patterned to fit the orders of a divorce decree that gave her mother sole custody. Every other weekend and one night a week was to be spent with her father. This was not always convenient for Mary or for her parents, but they tried to follow the arrangement as much as possible. Sometimes, Mary traded weekends at the request of her father. Sometimes she changed the schedule because of her own plans. She especially dreaded the Wednesday overnight visits. She would have to take the bus to her father's apartment on the far side of town and then get up early the next morning for the long ride back to school in time for her first class. Mary really enjoyed seeing her father, but she wished her parents still lived in the same house.

When Mary's father had to go away for six months she felt guilty about being glad, at first. It meant she would be able to forget about the weekend visits and the inconvenience of Wednesday night. Two weeks after her father had left, however, Mary wished he would come home again so she could talk to him. He had always understood how difficult it was for Mary to visit him and was always ready to spend time listening to her problems. Long before the six months were up, Mary was looking forward to getting back to the old schedule.

"Disneyland Dad"

Melissa spent one weekend a month with her father, a man who confused love with presents. Each time he came for her he had a new surprise. The whole weekend seemed spent in going to the zoo or the amusement park, the movies, or some other place her father thought she would like. The visits were full of excitement, but there was a great deal of tension, and this made Melissa feel uncomfortable. Going places was fun, but she would have preferred spending some of the time with her father, fixing her bicycle with him or just shopping together for a new pair of sneakers. She wished they could entertain each other by just talking, rather than always being entertained by someone or something else. Sometimes it almost seemed that her father was trying to buy her affection. Melissa hoped someday to have the courage to ask her father if they could just spend some quiet days together, even if she had to take the chance of hurting his feelings.

Actually, Melissa's father was exhausted after each visit. He would have welcomed a quiet day with her in which they could exchange opinions, talk about interests they shared, and act more naturally.

Making an appointment to be with a parent can be very artificial, and it is easy to understand why some parents wonder how they can best spend the short time they have with their children. Visitation is a time for parent and child to be with each other and enjoy each other. Although it is sometimes helpful to include a friend on a visit with a "weekend parent," time alone for discussing things can help to keep a positive relationship. Giving a father or a mother the chance to extend themselves can help to make visits more meaningful.

One father said that the nicest birthday present he ever received was his son's offer to spend a day with him doing whatever the father wanted. Children who spend an allotted time with one parent often find that such offers help to convert a "Disneyland Dad" into a better one.

Joint Custody

Karen is a 50-50 child—50 percent of the time is spent in her mother's home and 50 percent of the time in her father's. Someone asked her if she felt like a Ping-Pong ball. Actually, Karen's joint custody arrangement is working out very well, with half a week in two different homes that are just three miles apart. She keeps a separate set of clothing at each of the two apartments, she follows two sets of rules for watching television, getting to bed, and so forth, but she has one school and one set of friends. Karen is glad that her parents love her enough to let her love both of them and to spend part of her time with each one. She gives all her friends her schedule and both telephone numbers, so they know where to reach her all the time. In some ways, having two homes is fun for Karen.

Joint custody is not always so practical. For example, if parents live far from each other, or if there is no bedroom for a child in one home, such an arrangement can be difficult, if not impossible. Some children spend six months with one parent and six months with the other. Much of the success of sharing custody depends on the ability of parents to put aside their post-divorce resentments.

Consider the case of Jill and Rob. When their parents were divorced two years ago, their mother was awarded custody. Then their father decided he wanted to see them for more than their usual short visits, and he applied for a change in the custody arrangement, asking for joint custody. The mother said the father was a gambler and an inattentive father who abused his children. He described himself as devoted and responsible. He said the mother was a woman who hung around bars, picked up men, and brought them home for the night. She described herself as a homebody.

No matter who was right, such a joint custody request would be refused. According to those specialists who favor joint custody, it can only be helpful to the children when the parents do not harbor ill feelings toward each other. These parents were so embittered they could not be expected to make responsible decisions while sharing the physical care of their children.

The success of joint custody depends on the ability of parents to bury their hostilities and separate their feelings for their children from their feelings for each other. One couple who had an unfriendly divorce had a seven-year custody battle that was resolved by a joint custody arrangement, which appeared to be an unlikely solution at the time. The daughter was six months old when the parents separated. For the next seven years, the girl's mother had denied visitation rights to the father many times and the father had taken the matter to court many times. The girl, who is eight, now lives with each parent for half the week and seems much happier. Even her mother, who was against the new arrangement at the beginning, admits that the child has stopped stuttering and twitching. There seems no doubt that the best interests of the child were served in this case.

Since joint custody means sharing the major responsibilities for rearing and caring for children as well as making everyday decisions, there are times when it has proved both difficult and dangerous. For example, one child was placed in a difficult position when the mother wanted to send him to a certain school and the father blocked this by legal action. In another case, the parents could not agree on whether or not to allow a surgical operation.

Children as a Weapon

Unfortunately, the hostility between parents can be so great that they will use their child in a spiteful way. Linda's mother was badly hurt when her husband chose to move out of the house to live with another woman. Even though Linda was only three at the time, she had a very close relationship with her father, and she missed his daily attention and warmth.

Linda's mother loved her, but something as minor as a glass of spilled milk could cause a scene that was followed by severe punishment. Her mother felt that the little girl was always making a mess, and the household chores seemed endless. She seldom spent any time enjoying Linda; she was far more concerned with how the child was dressed and how she could prevent her from cluttering the house.

Although Linda's mother was awarded sole custody, her father had visiting rights and came to see his daughter as often as he could. Her mother resented these visits so much that she spoke to her lawyer about trying to stop them. She claimed that the father frightened the child. (This was one way she could punish her husband for the way he had left them.) An evaluation was suggested before the parents' lawyers brought the case before a judge so that therapists could determine whether or not the claim that Linda's father frightened Linda was really true. The mother insisted the child could not sleep after the father had visited, because he upset her. The father claimed that Linda enjoyed his visits and benefited from them.

Since Linda was not old enough to enter into any discussion of her feelings, it was decided to place the child in a playroom all by herself for a little while. The therapists could watch her from the next room through a one-way pane of glass.

Linda's mother and father entered the room at separate times. When her mother appeared, the therapists saw that Linda continued to play with the dolls in the dollhouse. When her mother left and her father entered the room, Linda ran to him and threw her arms around him. Certainly, this contradicted the kind of relationship that the mother had described.

Later, a psychiatrist asked Linda to play with the

dolls in a dollhouse. There was a mother doll, a father doll, and a little girl. As she played, Linda placed the little girl with the father and kept the mother in a different part of the house.

On the basis of these sessions, further tests, and discussions, Linda's mother was persuaded to permit the child's relationship with her father to continue. Through a long period of therapy, her mother was helped to relate to Linda in a more positive way and to understand that the sleepless nights after the father's visits might be caused partly by her own feelings of anxiety and hostility that were picked up by her daughter.

Children as an Ego Trip

George hated to visit his father, but he was made to spend every other weekend at his father's house. Actually, he never really spent time with his father. His father would take him along to his club, where George would swim and read while his father played golf. At the end of the day they would go back to his father's house, where George would eat some fried chicken or a hamburger from the take-out store down the street. His father would dress for dinner while George was eating, and then he would either go out or entertain some adults, leaving George to watch television alone. The next day's routine was much the same, with each person going his own way.

George often tried to stay home with his friends rather than spend the weekend at his father's house, but his father refused to give up the arrangement. George couldn't see what difference it made to his father. He never suspected his father took pride in his power to keep George away from his former wife when she wanted her son at home.

Children as Spies

Don was uncomfortable about going from one parent to the other because both parents used him as a spy. When he was with his mother, she inquired about what his father did in his new living quarters. She was curious about how he spent his free time, whether or not he was dating any women, what they were like, and how much money he spent on them. Don's father asked questions about his mother's friends, how much she drank and smoked, and where she slept. Don tried to please each parent by giving as many answers as he could, but he felt as if he was always in the middle. Besides, he did not really like himself for spying. Actually, his parents were using him to help continue their fighting. When Don asked the school counselor what he could do about this, she suggested that he refuse to answer questions about the other parent. She told him that no one respects a spy since such a person cannot be trusted with a secret.

Don found that after he took a firm stand with each parent, the questions stopped. He felt much better about himself when the spying ended.

Custody Fights

Most states today have ratified the Uniform Child Custody Act, whereby a state agrees to honor the child custody orders of other states. Before this happened, however, there were many battles over custody.

Judy's parents were divorced when she was seven years old and she was placed in the custody of her mother, who lived in New York State. By choice, she spent summers with her father in Vermont. When she was nine years old, Judy's father decided not to send her back to her mother in time for school but to fight for the custody of his daughter.

Judy's mother tried to contact her without success. No one would answer her questions, and when she called the father's house she was referred to a lawyer. No one asked Judy if she wanted to go back to her mother and the school she had attended the year before; her father just decided he wanted to keep her with him. He took the case to court and filed legal papers claiming that his wife was not a fit mother because she was under the constant care of a psychiatrist, even though this was untrue. Judy was enrolled in a school near her father's home and entered the first day of the fall term as if she would be staying for the full year.

In the meantime Judy's mother also hired a lawyer, who issued a warrant for the arrest of Judy's father, because he had interfered with the custody order that was issued at the time of the divorce in New York. However, the warrant was useless unless her father appeared in New York since out-of-state custody orders did not then apply in Vermont.

Judy's mother, who was not at all unfit to care for the child as her former husband had claimed, was told by her lawyer to go to Vermont and take Judy home with her. But the mother worried about what this would do to Judy. She did drive up and check with the principal to see if her daughter was really attending school and to ask if the child was well. Since both things appeared to be true, the mother returned home to wait for the court hearing.

Two months went by. At last there was a hearing before a judge. Judy's mother did not see her daughter in the courthouse (where she had been brought by her father's lawyer) until Judy took the stand and was asked to choose between her parents. The father had already tried to persuade Judy to choose him. The judge refused to allow a nine-year-old to speak in the presence of two hostile parents. He took the girl to his chambers, where he had a private conversation with the child. He had already read that the father's allegation that the mother was unfit was untrue. Two weeks later, Judy's mother was notified that the judge upheld the New York decree and she could take her daughter home with her permanently.

Although Judy was glad to return to her old home and school, she felt confused by the whole experience. Even though her father had been wrong, she would miss her summer visits with him. In Judy's case, as in most custody fights, the child is the big loser.

If the Uniform Child Custody Act had been in effect in all states when Judy's parents were fighting for her custody, her father would not have been able to keep her away so long.

An increasing number of families are working out custody problems with the help of people who are impartial. Therapists employed by the court do custody evaluations, and custody investigators do family studies and interview teachers, neighbors, and friends to help determine the living arrangement that is best for each child. In many states, a guardian is appointed for a child in an effort to represent the child's point of view and to be objective in the emotional times of determining the best custody situation. In Wisconsin, the court is required by law to appoint an attorney for the child in a contested custody case.

Fortunately, most parents are able to resolve the problems of custody without seriously draining their financial and emotional resources on court costs. About 90 percent of child custody arrangements are settled without serious battles in which a judge has to decide the question of who gets custody of the children. One hopes that in all cases the needs of the children are considered first.

Parental Kidnapping

A growing number of parents are snatching their children from the parent who has custody and fleeing with them to far places. Some cases of parental kidnapping sound like spy stories. Parents and children have been known to escape the custodial parent by flying away in small planes, using false passports to hide in foreign countries, bribing foreign bureaucrats, and adopting elaborate disguises.

Sometimes a young child who has been kidnapped by a parent is unaware of what has happened, at least for the first few weeks. This was the case for David, a four-year-old boy whose Italian father was an international businessman. David thought the flight from New York to Rome with his father was the beginning of a vacation in which he would spend some time with his father's family in Italy. As the weeks stretched on, David began to realize that this was not just a vacation.

His mother, an attorney in New York, started court proceedings, which led to the return of the boy in four and a half months. Not all children are returned this fast, and some never go back to the parent from whom they were stolen.

No one knows how many children are abducted by parents who do not have custody. Estimates run as high as 600,000 in the United States each year, but the true figure is probably much lower. Many children are taken across state lines, and an increasing number are taken across national boundaries. Mrs. Rodriguez was living in California when her former husband took their eight-year-old twins to Argentina. This mother sold her house, borrowed $250,000 to pay lawyers and detectives to help get the boys away from their father, and went to Argentina. Three years after the children were taken, a judge in Argentina signed an order that permitted

Mrs. Rodriguez to take them back to the United States. She and the boys fled in a small plane immediately for fear the father would file an appeal that would detain them.

Very few people can afford large fees for detectives and lawyers in a private search for their stolen children. The police seldom help when cases are reported to them, because it is difficult to prove that there is a crime when the children are taken by a parent. Even the FBI cannot help in many child-snatching cases. However, there have actually been cases in which people without a great deal of money were able to locate and rescue their children. Ruth Livingston's case was one of them.

Mrs. Livingston lived in California with her toddlers, Jimmy and Sally. She had worked out an arrangement with another mother of young children to look after them while she worked. Although she was not legally divorced from her husband, she had started the proceedings and had asked for custody of the children. She tried to keep her whereabouts secret because her husband had been abusive. He managed to find her, however, and to steal the children by forcing his way into the place where they were living. He had two friends pose as police officers who demanded that the children go with their father. The baby-sitter was so frightened and confused that the father had a two-hour start before the mother learned what had happened. Even then, the police could not have arrested him since he was the children's father and there had been no broken custody agreement.

Eighteen months went by. During this time, Mrs. Livingston did not know where her children were or even whether they were safe and healthy. Then she had a lead about where the children might be. As a result of an application she made out for a loan at the bank, she discovered that her husband had overdrawn money from a joint account that she had shared with him. The bank traced him to a city in Texas. The telephone company was able to give her his phone number, so she dialed it, heard his voice, and hung up without telling him who she was.

Then things began to happen. The next day, her divorce was granted and she was given custody of the children. And the following day, Mrs. Livingston and her father drove to the city in Texas where her former husband was living. Here she learned that neither the police nor the local district attorney's office would help, but they promised not to stop her from taking the children back home with her. After a period of confusion, the children went back happily to their former home in California with their mother, who had the legal right to care for them.

Although childnapping by a father appears to be more common than by a mother, there are also many cases in which a mother takes the children illegally. In either type of situation, the problems usually take a long time to resolve. For example, one mother of a two-year-old disappeared with her daughter after she lost custody to the father because she refused to let him visit the child. It was two years before the father succeeded in bringing his child back from a neighboring state.

What causes parental kidnapping? In many cases, child snatching occurs because one parent refuses to allow the other to see the child. Sometimes one parent feels that the other parent is making unfair financial demands. The belief that judges are unfair in being more likely to give mothers custody of young children than fathers is thought to be behind some cases of parental kidnapping. The consequences hurt both parents and children no matter what the motives. In one tragic case, a father and son were killed in a car crash when they were being chased by the child's mother.

Few people can appreciate the extent of the emotional damage to children who are kidnapped by parents and hidden under cover of moving from place to place. They live constantly in a tension-filled situation, which sometimes lasts for years. In one case, two children were taken by their mother from their father in Michigan. The mother settled with them in New York, where the father located them and appealed to the court. They lived with their mother for three years, during which court appeals moved slowly through the legal process. In the end, they moved back to Michigan to custody of their father, but during the time they were gone, both the children and their old environment had changed a great deal.

The problems of missing and exploited children first came to the forefront of public attention with the disappearance of Etan Patz. This little boy never reached the place two blocks from his New York home where he would have caught the bus for his first-grade class on the morning of May 25, 1979. His disappearance set off one of the most extensive manhunts in history.

The tragedy of Adam Walsh occurred about two years later, when he was abducted from a Florida department store where he had been shopping with his mother. When the remains of this six-year-old boy were found in a canal, people far and wide were shocked. Later, Adam Walsh's story reached more than fifty million people when it appeared in the form of a television movie. It depicted, in part, some of the work his parents did to alert the federal government to the need for help. Their testimony played a part in the passage of the Missing Children Act of 1982.

Other media publicity connected with a series of child murders in Atlanta and the murders of a number of runaway children in Texas in the early 1980s helped to increase concern about the seriousness of the general problem of missing children.

Although the abduction of children by strangers is probably not as prevalent as it was once believed to be, it is still a tremendous and terrible tragedy. A much larger tragedy is the number of missing children who are abducted by parents who do not have custody.

Many children who have been kidnapped report that they feel like baggage being carried from city to city. They never stay long in one school or home, so they never really have a chance to make lasting friendships. These children are often made to use aliases, live under the guard of detectives, and lie to authorities. Many suffer great emotional pain, longing for the parent from whom they have been taken. So even though parental kidnapping may not seem serious to law enforcement agencies, it is both serious and tragic for those directly involved. With rare exceptions, parental kidnapping is a destructive act on the part of the parent who does the kidnapping.

A measure to deter child snatching passed Congress without debate and was signed into law by President Carter during Christmas week of 1980. The law ordered the Federal Bureau of Investigation to use its resources to help locate parents who take their children across state lines after arrest warrants have been issued. It also increased cooperation between states. (Formerly some had refused to cooperate with each other on custody cases unless children were in physical danger.)

Although some progress has been made in helping custodial parents locate children who have been kidnapped, much remains to be done. The establishment of the National Center for Missing and Exploited Children was a tremendous step forward. In addition to providing help in locating children, this government organization helps to educate the public about the true nature of the missing children situation and researches a wide variety of connected problems.

Many of the developments in the area are new. For example, mothers who kidnap their children to protect them from the sexual abuse by fathers are growing in number. A number of safe houses shelter them as they move from place to place, somewhat the way houses hid runaway slaves at the time of the Civil War. In some cases, the reasons for abducting a child are based on problems that are unrecognized by the courts, which continue to permit visits by the guilty father. However, there are mothers who use the charge of sexual abuse falsely in attempting to discredit their husbands' or ex-husbands' bids for custody or visiting rights. When accusations are proven false, children are sometimes removed from the custody of their mothers and placed with their fathers, but false allegations are hard to prove. Mothers of young children may teach them to parrot comments in efforts to prove sexual abuse. Parents who resort to such techniques harm their children emotionally. Doctors and social workers are studying ways to differentiate between false and actual allegations of sexual abuse in the hope of preventing such emotional harm to children and parents.

People from all walks of life have become involved in trying to make life better for children who are victims of parental kidnapping. Many private organizations help to find abducted children, using volunteers who contribute time and money. Although the National Center for Missing and Exploited Children has helped to find over 8,000 children and assisted in the investigation of over 15,000 cases since it was founded in 1984, much remains to be done. An overwhelming number of children remain on the list of those who are missing, and more names will be added to it in the future.

No one knows how many parental kidnappings take place each year. Efforts to prevent child snatching will be important until this abuse is no longer a threat to any children.

5

Living in Stepfamilies

Cindy sat glowering on the steps of the house belonging to the man her mother had just married and watched the empty moving van drive away. She really hated this house, even though her desk, her books, her bicycle, and most of her other possessions were in this place that was to be her new home. She had her own room, a room that was larger than the one in the old house, but it would never be the same. She missed her friends, her old school, the park where she used to play, and just about everything.

"Hello." A friendly voice interrupted her musing. A short, stout woman stood in front of her. "Are you Mr. King's new little girl?"

Cindy shook her head, even though she knew that Mr. King was now her stepfather. Cindy was sure he could never replace her father. She would never be his little girl.

Cindy is just one of many children who experience hostility when parents remarry. They see the stepparent as a permanent intrusion in the relationship with their remaining natural parent and as an end to the hope that their divorced parents might someday remarry. Cindy was not one of the fortunate children who could talk with her stepfather about her feelings. Her stepfather did not know how to make her understand that he would not compete with her father, or how to explain that his place in her life would be unique and different from her relationship with her father. He knew he was an additional parent; he did not think of himself as a replacement. Nor did her mother.

Many people enter into stepfamily relationships with the idea that relationships will fall into place and be the same as in the original families. They are optimistic, but they are unaware of the many different feelings that must be resolved.

About one in six American children below the age of eighteen lives in a stepfamily, and by the year 2000 this may be one child in four. These families differ in many ways from the biological family into which most of us are born. All these individuals come together with ghosts from the past, with good ways and bad ways of doing and feeling. Most come with mixed feelings about their new situations.

Suppose you are getting another mother as a result of your father's remarriage. Technically, she is your stepmother, but you can't call her that when you speak to her. Just finding the most comfortable name for this new member of your family may be difficult. You probably do not want to call her "Mother," especially if your own mother is alive. But you might feel comfortable with a variation of the name you use for your own mother. You might call her by her first name. This is a common solution, but some stepmothers feel it puts them in a bad position when there is a need to discipline. Many stepmothers are called aunt along with their first names. Others like to be called Mom June, or a similar combination of a name for mother and their own names. As mentioned in chapter 1, even stepfamilies are called by many names, such as blended families, reconstituted families, and reorganized families.

The Cruel Stepmother Myth

The whole idea of a stepmother comes with built-in problems, partly because of stories that are told to young children. The stepmothers in legends and fairy tales have traditionally been wicked. Cinderella's stepmother is well known for making her stepchild work at dirty tasks while the rest of the family went to the ball. One young child was terrified of joining a stepfamily in which she would have two older stepsisters because she imagined herself being treated like Cinderella.

Most children are familiar with other tales of cruel stepmothers. Snow White's stepmother was reassured each day when she consulted her mirror that she was the most beautiful of all. Then one day the mirror told her that her stepdaughter, Snow White, was now the fairest. The stepmother solved this problem by having Snow White taken out into the woods to be put to death. In the end, Snow White marries a handsome prince and her stepmother is the one who dies.

The stepmother in "Hansel and Gretel" is famous for her cruelty, too. When there was not enough food to go around, the stepchildren were sent away to fend for themselves in the woods. They killed the witch (who symbolizes the cruel stepmother) and returned home to find that their stepmother had died.

In the story "The Juniper Tree," the cruel stepmother cuts the stepchild into pieces for soup and serves it to the father, who eats it.

The myth of the cruel stepmother is one of the factors that makes a good relationship difficult. In real life, stories about stepmothers tend to be cruel, too. Even though they are objects of hostility, the great majority of stepmothers try very hard to be good in their new roles. Some of them may be hindered because they try too hard.

The Myth of Instant Love

Twelve-year-old Joan and her father felt very close after her mother left them. They depended on each other as friends. Joan's first reaction was one of jealousy when her father's new wife, Bonnie, came into the picture. Joan developed headaches when Bonnie was around. Bonnie, on the other hand, was very self-assured. She played games with Joan, took her shopping, and did many favors for her new stepdaughter. She was sure she could win her over, but somehow she lacked sensitivity. Actually, Bonnie tried so hard she made things more difficult.

Bonnie rearranged her own schedule to fit Joan's. She tried to anticipate the girl's needs and satisfy her wants even when they seemed unreasonable. Still Joan was resistant. Trying to be the perfect stepmother became exhausting for Bonnie.

Joan did not appreciate Bonnie's special efforts to please her, and Bonnie got upset because she tried so hard and still did not win her new daughter's love.

The myth of the cruel stepmother is no more prevalent than the myth of instant love. Many women who are about to become instant mothers to the children of the men they marry feel that they will be able to win the child's affection quickly. Sometimes this feeling is encouraged by good relationships before marriage. The father and his future new wife go on outings with his children and have many enjoyable times. But it is typical for the good times to stop when the actual marriage takes place.

Experts who work with the problems of stepfamilies state again and again that it is unrealistic to expect stepchildren and stepparents to love each other immediately upon formation of the new family. Even the impression that they *must* love each other can be harmful. Just because a woman loves a man, it does not follow that she will immediately love his children. Even those children who think they love a person who is going to become a stepparent discover that living together is very different from sharing outings and trips to the movies. It takes a long time for love to grow between people even when there are no complicated feelings involved, as there are in the case of stepfamilies.

Stepparents and stepchildren find it helpful to know that they should not be expected to love each other immediately. The family can be happy as long as there is respect and consideration for each of its members. Both children and parents need time to adjust, accept, and belong. Love is often a bonus that comes later.

Loyalty

One of the feelings that gets in the way of a good relationship with a stepparent is loyalty. Suppose the natural mother has died. The children remember her as a wonderful person. In fact, they tend to idealize her. This new mother can never replace their own mother, nor should she expect to do this.

When Penny's father remarried, Penny assembled all the pictures she could find of her mother, who had died when Penny was four years old. Now that she was eight, Penny remembered only the happy days they had had together. Actually, Penny's mother had been so depressed she took her own life. Penny's father had never told Penny about this, for he wanted her to remember her early childhood days as happy and think of her mother as a caring person.

Penny's father was especially happy with his new wife, who was good-humored and easygoing. She tried to understand Penny's feelings of loyalty to her mother and helped the girl frame some of her mother's pictures. Even with this understanding, it took many years before Penny could feel close to this new mother. On some days, she felt that she hated her father for neglecting his first wife's memory. But on other days, she felt contented to be close to a mature older woman who could listen to her problems and care for her needs.

When a natural mother dies, psychologists believe that the children harbor some resentment toward her for having abandoned them, even though they are aware of the fact that in the majority of cases, and unlike Penny's mother, she had no control over her death. Since this hostility cannot be expressed openly, the stepmother may serve as a target for it.

When a mother and a stepmother are both part of a child's family, loyalties can be difficult too. There is naturally some rivalry between the biological mother and the stepmother for the children's affection. The natural mother resents the actions of the stepmother, no matter how well intentioned they may be. Put in a position of divided loyalty, the children usually side with their natural mothers. They feel guilty if they like or love their stepmothers. When children realize that some of their problems in relating to their stepmothers are partly due to these loyalty conflicts, their hostile feelings are usually less strong. Children need to be reminded again and again that the relationship with stepparents is different from the relationship with natural parents. A stepparent does not replace the natural parent, but, rather acts as an additional parent.

Sharing a Parent

Having a new stepparent means sharing a natural parent. Many children feel that the stepparent is going to take the love of their remaining parent away completely, so they will lose him or her. For some children, remarriage means losing one's place as an only child or as the eldest or the youngest child. It is easier if children can express the anxieties and doubts that are felt when a stepparent enters the family. Everyone has some of these feelings, for there are changes with which everyone must cope.

Before her mother remarried, Carol felt she had a very special place in her mother's life. Afterward, her stepfather took a great deal of her mother's free time. Carol decided to go to her room every day when she came home from school, and she refused to eat dinner at the table with her stepfather. Carol was sullen and withdrawn, isolating herself from the family in every possible way. She continued this behavior for several months. She knew she was jealous of her stepfather, but she did not realize that part of the problem was anger at her mother, for having betrayed her by bringing this new person into the family, and fear that she would lose her special place in her mother's heart. It was almost a year before Carol began to accept her stepfather and make a little room for this additional person. Eventually she discovered that he even added some good things to her life.

We Do It This Way Here

At some time or other, most stepmothers hear the words, "You are not my mother. You have no right to tell me what to do."

When his wife died, Mr. Blair retired so that he could take care of his three teenage daughters. He devoted all his time to cooking for them, driving them to their activities, and providing for their needs. He grew more and more lonesome as the girls grew older and spent an increasing amount of their time with their friends. Gradually, Mr. Blair formed a good relationship with a woman whose name was Barbara, who had been divorced for a long time. He and Barbara decided to marry, and Barbara moved into the Blair home.

The girls disliked sharing their father with his new wife. They tried to accept Barbara as an older friend and as a member of the family but found it very difficult after having had their father to themselves. Barbara felt that her new husband waited on the girls too much. They were used to having him serve the meals and clean up afterward. Now Barbara was serving the meals, but she expected the girls to do the dishes and told them so. They reacted by telling her that she had no right to give them orders. Unfortunately, their father did not support Barbara in her request but, rather, helped her with the chores she asked the girls to do. Mealtime conversation consisted of asking for the salt or a second helping of food. Barbara, who thought she would enjoy having company at mealtime after living alone for many years, felt frustrated in her attempts to make pleasant conversation. If Mr. Blair had discussed the rules of the house with Barbara before they were married and supported her in some of her requests, the marriage would have been more pleasant for everyone.

In many families, there is confusion because children who live alternately with two sets of parents may find there are two sets of rules. In the Russell household, the stepmother responds to "My mother does it this way" with "In this house, we do it differently." For example, bedtime is 11 P.M. at the natural mother's house and 10 P.M. at the Russell house. Mrs. Russell holds firm to her rules, insisting that in this house the children go to bed at 10 P.M. The same holds true about chores, mealtime rules, and picking up clothing. Mrs. Russell knows that children feel more secure when they understand what is expected of them and know that someone cares enough to see that they follow the rules of the house.

Many stepparents feel timid about disciplining children who are not theirs, while others plunge in with extremely rigid rules. It helps if stepparents are aware of the need to be flexible and understanding.

Kinds of Love

Many stepparents grow to love the children from former marriages as much as they would ever love children who were born to them. In some cases, where a natural parent shows no interest in a child, adoption seems to be a happy arrangement for all the people involved.

One stepfather who had adopted his wife's daughter by a former marriage fought the Unification Church for five years because he claimed that they had exercised mind control techniques in recruiting her and depriving him of his parental rights. This stepfather insisted he was willing to "give up everything" to get his adopted daughter back from the church group she had chosen to live with instead of her family.

Sometimes children are appalled to discover that they may stimulate their new stepparents or stepbrothers and stepsisters sexually if they wander around the house in various stages of undress as has been their custom.

One stepfather found that he felt very uncomfortable when his stepdaughters continued to live as casually as they had before he joined the family. He suggested that the girls wear robes when they were not fully dressed and that they all respect one another's privacy. Sometimes a stepfather and stepdaughter are attracted to each other in a sexual way. This situation is often helped by a professional therapist.

Many cases of runaway girls involve stepfathers who sexually abuse them. Most stepfathers are not guilty of this kind of behavior, but if you feel uneasy about a situation of this kind, discuss it with your own parent. If this does not lead to the help you need, contact a local mental health center or other place in the list called Where to Get Help at the end of this book.

Stepbrothers and Stepsisters

Many children of remarried parents find themselves sharing a house with boys or girls who are children of the stepparent. In one household where the parents had combined their furniture and dishes, the children showed definite preference for the things that had come from their original homes. In all cases, people bring old habits and behavior from their previous family life. Sometimes, different ways of doing things cause conflicts. It helps if the family can realize that everyone has to make adjustments.

Jealousy is common in families where the children are "his" and "hers" and in cases where there are new children by the remarriage. Often a father feels guilty because he spends more time with his stepchildren than with his own children because of the living arrangement. When stepbrothers and stepsisters live together, there is often jealousy about a natural parent's favoritism or over attention paid to stepchildren. Few families blend as easily as on the popular TV shows, where all problems seem to be solved by the end of a half-hour program.

Many stepfamilies work out their difficulties by discussing roles and rules at family conferences. Each one tries to put himself or herself in the shoes of everyone else involved in the stepfamily relationship and to understand how the other members of the family are feeling. This is not easy. Instant families seldom find instant harmony, but it helps to know that people in stepfamilies have special feelings and need not feel guilty about many of the negative ones.

In most stepfamilies, people are happier if they understand that stepfamilies are different from natural families and that everyone has to try a little harder. Children who can discuss their feelings have an easier time making room for three or four parents in their lives. Although there are times when stepchildren are lonely and unhappy about the divorce of their parents, many of them are able to find good things about having a stepparent.

6

Other Kinds of Families

Individuals who are not related by biological ties may nevertheless have close ties to one another. Such groups can be defined as families in an emotional sense.

The Institution as Family

At eighteen years of age, Aggie was definitely odd-looking. She was barely five feet tall, with a pasty complexion, straggly hair, and pale-blue staring eyes. Her front teeth were crooked and protruding and she had a small receding chin, which made her resemble a rabbit. It was difficult to understand her speech, because her voice was high-pitched and nasal, and she slurred her words. Aggie had been in the state mental hospital for five years. Everyone on the staff knew her, and she knew them. She had become a kind of pet, and people were accustomed to her unusual appearance and to her behavior. She often acted like a small child, making unreasonable demands, trying to wheedle favors, sneaking food, doing mischief, or throwing herself on the floor in a temper tantrum if she could not get her way. Sometimes she became so upset and depressed she pulled out her hair or cut herself. She always had complaints about physical problems—stomach pains, headaches, cough—and occasionally she swallowed objects like pins or buttons. Aggie always made sure the staff paid extra attention to her, and she was ingenious about thinking up ways to get it.

None of the psychiatrists and psychologists agreed about what was wrong with Aggie. Her mother was an alcoholic and, during most of Aggie's early childhood, had been either in treatment centers or too befogged with drink to pay much attention to her daughter. The father hadn't spent much time at home, and when he was there, he and his wife had terrible fights. All the children in the family were afraid of him. Eventually, Aggie and her brothers and sisters were placed in foster homes because their parents were neglecting them. Unfortunately, Aggie went from one foster home to another. No one wanted her because she was such a difficult child. She was awkward, she was a slow learner, it was hard to understand her speech, and she was very unattractive. Everyone ignored her. Finally, they decided she must be retarded, and she was placed in a home for retarded people. She stayed there for several years, until her behavior became disruptive and she was transferred to the mental institution. Now she was considered mentally ill as well as retarded, and no one thought she would ever change.

But one of the social workers at the hospital chose Aggie as his special project, and he and some of the other staff worked out a plan for encouraging her to show more acceptable behavior. She responded to their support and praise and finally began to feel that perhaps there was something likable about herself. She became very attached to the head nurse on the ward, whom she called "Aunt Betty." Aunt Betty sometimes took her home on weekends or went with her on outings to buy trinkets and eat at the fast-food restaurant in the shopping mall.

Aggie became quite content at the hospital. She would roam around, visiting friends on other wards, or walk downtown and buy a soda at the coffee shop, where everyone knew her. She enjoyed having literally dozens of people who worked at the hospital greet her by name. She felt she really belonged at last. In fact, when her social worker and psychiatrist suggested that perhaps now she might be ready to leave the hospital and live in a small group home in the community, Aggie became very upset. She wanted to stay in the place she considered home, and she wanted to remain with the people she considered her family. Life in the community, in her experience, had been full of rejections, abuse, and disappointments. Neither her own parents nor her foster parents had been consistent or reliable, and she no longer trusted anyone out there.

It might seem unbelievable that someone would actually prefer to remain in an institution, in the company of individuals who exhibit disturbed or unusual behavior, and in a setting that many would consider rather grim. Nevertheless, there are many people like Aggie, for whom an institution has become a comfortable home where staff and inmates form a supportive family.

Maybe if Aggie had been persuaded to visit the group home, she would have understood that it, too, was a kind of family. It was an old house in a residential neighborhood, where five or six young adults lived with an older couple who acted as houseparents. The young people were all moderately retarded, and some had physical handicaps. They needed help and supervision, but they were able to do almost everything that people without handicaps do and enjoy. They shared in the chores, including shopping, cleaning, and cooking. All of them had part-time jobs or went regularly to a special center where they participated in activities. These people had special needs and could not live with their own families. Some had no family; others were unwelcome or clashed with parents or siblings. The houseparents and other workers at the group home received special training and were qualified to handle most difficulties, and they were patient and caring. Aggie probably would have felt comfortable as a member of this little family group if she had joined it.

Foster Families

Four-year-old Tanya was placed temporarily with a foster family because her mother and stepfather were drug addicts and could not care for her properly. After six months, Tanya's mother completed a drug treatment program and went back to school part-time. She also left her husband because he refused treatment for his addiction. Now she wanted her daughter back, and the social worker assigned to the case agreed that Tanya's mother was ready to be a good parent. However, Tanya's foster family had become very attached to her in the meantime and wanted to keep her. They argued that they would be able to give Tanya a much better life. She would have all the advantages of an upper-middle-class home: such things as dancing lessons, ski trips, and private school. If Tanya were returned to her mother, she would grow up in a single-parent disadvantaged family in a poor neighborhood. She would certainly never receive the material and cultural enrichment that the foster family could provide.

The judge who heard this case decided that Tanya's mother had really changed her lifestyle and was a good and caring parent. He therefore ordered that Tanya be returned to her mother, despite the advantages that she might have had with the foster family.

Sometimes, removing a child from his or her natural parents is necessary, and even judges and mental health professionals have a difficult time predicting what the best living situation would be. Caring foster families can be a solution for children like Tanya who need temporary placement in a secure and stable environment.

Gay and Lesbian Parents

Many people believe that homosexuals are antifamily and have no interest in being parents. You may be surprised to know that on the contrary, gays and lesbians often want children just as heterosexual men and women do, and they create families that may not look any different from ordinary families. A homosexual may be married to a heterosexual woman and they may have children, for instance. And some lesbians and gay men adopt children, either as single parents or with a lover.

Some research has shown that from 3 to 5 percent of the adult male population is gay in almost all cultures that have been surveyed, including the United States, although other studies have indicated a higher percentage of homosexual men in this country. Some of these men have been married. According to some estimates, there may be as many as two or three million gay men who are natural fathers.

Gay men marry for many of the same reasons that most people want to get married: for love and companionship. Some are unaware of their homosexuality at the time of marriage. Others may think that getting married will overcome their homosexual tendencies. Some men may be bisexual (that is, attracted to both men and women). Although some couples stay together because of their children, most of these marriages are likely to end in divorce. The gay fathers then usually become more openly involved with other gay men.

Gay fathers may discover that their life is made

more difficult and complicated because of their children, but most remain loving and concerned parents. However, having come out of the closet, as it is called, they may not be accepted by either the straight community or the gay community. (One expert has called this "the double closet.") Gays who are not parents themselves may not understand the importance of being a parent.

The numbers of families involving lesbian mothers and gay fathers seem to be increasing, and some studies show that there may be 6 to 14 million children of gay or lesbian parents. Do those children become homosexuals? Do they develop emotional disturbances? These are questions that concern many people, and researchers are beginning to find some answers.

The idea that gay parents influence their children to become gay is a myth. There is no research to support this theory. One expert has asked, "Who are the parents of gay human beings?" The answer is that the majority of homosexuals have heterosexual parents.

On the other hand, psychiatrists at Boston University have found some evidence that male homosexuality seems to run in families. In a study of 51 homosexual men and 50 heterosexual men, the researchers discovered that only 4 percent of the brothers of the heterosexuals were homosexual, but 18 percent of the brothers of the homosexuals were homosexual. They found no differences among the sisters. The researchers emphasized that their study could not show whether heredity or environment played a more important role.

Another prevalent fear is that gay or lesbian parents may seduce their children, but in fact, that risk is no higher than with heterosexual parents.

Concerns about children experiencing emotional problems because they live in gay or lesbian families are perhaps more realistic. Life can be difficult in a society that stigmatizes homosexuality. According to some researchers, most children are able to accept a parent's homosexuality, although initially they may react with confusion, worry, anger, or shock. Even if they disapprove of their parent's sexual orientation, most are able to accept the homosexual parent in the role of father or mother.

Some questions children may ask are: What makes a person homosexual? (No one really knows.) Did your lover persuade you to become homosexual? (No one can force someone else to change his or her feelings of sexual attraction.) Will I be homosexual? (It isn't catching, like a cold.)

Children are also concerned about what their friends and neighbors might think. One fourteen-year-old boy was upset with his father because he visited the boy's school wearing lots of jewelry, and the teachers and kids guessed that he was gay. They started calling the boy names, which made him feel very uncomfortable.

Some children who feel at odds with society can sympathize with a parent whose lifestyle differs from the norm. Sixteen-year-old Charlie said that he experienced other people's prejudice against him because of his obesity, just as his father felt stigmatized for his homosexuality. Another boy said he envied his father for being different.

Homosexual stepparents have some special problems because society does not recognize their role as legitimate. While a homosexual man may marry a woman who has a child and can even adopt the child, a lesbian lover may act as a stepparent, but she has no legal status. Bev and Jane lived together as lovers with Jane's eight-year-old daughter, Jenny. Although Jenny knew that Bev was supposed to be in charge of the household when Jane was away on business trips, she would rebel and misbehave while her mother was absent, saying Bev had no right to tell her what to do. Bev and Jane had told Jenny only that they were good friends, because they wanted to keep their lesbian relationship a secret. Their problem was how to get Jenny to accept Bev as a family member with some authority. They decided to seek counseling so they could work on ways to improve this relationship.

Many such families feel the need to keep their true relationships a secret from their children until they are old enough to understand what homosexuality means. They often conceal their identity from the rest of the world because of their fear of disapproval by the community. They may face the threat of eviction from their apartments, loss of employment, and loss of child custody.

Many people object strongly to the lifestyles of gays and lesbians, while others are more accepting. It is important to dispel some of the myths about homosexuals and to have some understanding of the problems of the children in these families.

The Street as Family

Fourteen-year-old Ginny decided to run away from home about a year after her mother remarried. Her stepfather, Tom, had never seemed to like the idea that he would have to take her if he wanted to marry her mother. It wasn't too bad at first, because Tom ignored Ginny most of the time, but after a few months he and Ginny's mother began to argue and fight often, especially after Tom had been drinking. The marriage was deteriorating, and finally Ginny's mother met another man and went off to live with him, leaving Ginny with Tom. Ginny did not know that this situation would be temporary. She was desperate because she believed she had nowhere to turn. She thought her mother didn't want her, and she was too ashamed to tell any relatives or friends. So one night she threw a few articles of clothing into her knapsack, went to the bus station, and bought a ticket to New York City. She arrived in New York feeling lonely and frightened and wandered down Forty-second Street, sneaking glances at the kids who were hanging around there. Many of them looked as though they were high on drugs. Some of the girls were smoking cigarettes nervously, pre- tending to be tougher and more self-confident than they really were. She noticed an older man trying to pick up a boy who appeared to be no more than twelve years old.

Tired and hungry, Ginny found a cheap all-night diner and sat down at the counter to eat a hamburg- er. Two girls who took the seats next to her asked her if she needed a place to stay and Ginny accepted their offer gladly. She discovered that they shared quarters with rats and cockroaches in an abandoned building that had no heat or running water. But at least it was a roof over her head, with people her own age who could understand why she had run away. She hung around with the girls and their friends for several weeks, hoping to find a way of earning money without resorting to prostitution.

Ginny's only family at that point in her life was this group of street kids. Some were unwed mothers whose families had thrown them out; others were delinquents, drug addicts, or school dropouts. Many had been shuttled around among various foster homes and institutions. They all shared a common bond; they were outsiders. Suspicious and angry toward everyone else, they felt unwanted, and they needed one another's companionship and support. There are more than a million kids in the streets today, and about two thirds of them are throwaways, children whose families do not want them back.

Life on the street is boring, but it can be dangerous as well. Assaults, rape, arrest, drug overdoses, AIDS, suicide, and murder take their toll, and more than 5,000 unidentified young people die every year.

Ginny knew she didn't want to end up like some of the kids she met, but she wasn't sure what to do. Then one day she saw a poster. It said AWAY FROM HOME? NEED HELP? and gave the telephone number of a toll-free twenty-four-hour hotline operated by the National Runaway Switchboard. When Ginny called the number, the woman who answered the phone told her that their conversation would be confidential. She asked Ginny if she needed medical attention or a place to stay. She said that Ginny could leave a message to be relayed to her family. Ginny replied that she needed somewhere to sleep but she didn't have any money. The hotline operator gave her the telephone number and address of Covenant House.

Covenant House and other shelters like it are safe places where runaways can stay for short periods of time. They are free and confidential. The staff does not notify parents unless they are asked to do so. They can refer people for medical attention or legal assistance, and they can help the individual decide what he or she would like to do. Ginny was greeted by friendly workers; she ate a good dinner and slept in a bed with clean sheets. The next morning, she asked a staff member to telephone her mother and leave a message saying she wanted to go home. Ginny's mother had been frantic with worry ever since Tom called her to say that Ginny had run away. She had also been feeling guilty that she hadn't taken Ginny with her right away instead of planning to send for her after she got settled in her new apartment. She wanted Ginny to leave New York that very day so they could be reunited as soon as possible.

Ginny was one of the fortunate kids whose story has a happy ending, but for most members of the street family, the endings are tragic.

The Religious Group as Family

Barry was twelve years old when his father was killed in a plane crash. Since his father was a famous politician, the media broadcast this event on the front pages of the papers and on television newscasts. Barry had little chance to talk to his mother, who was surrounded by friends and dignitaries. He was an only child who had been close to his father before politics entered the picture.

Barry's father was coming home to stay when the plane accident occurred. Barry was especially eager to see his father again, for he had no brothers or sisters and his father always made him feel special. He had waited a long time for the day when his father would leave the political scene and play tennis with him the way he did in the old days. That could never happen now. The future had changed, but Barry could not bring himself to really believe his father was dead. Although his mother tried to comfort him when she found time, that time was brief. Barry was alone.

The funeral for Barry's father was large and impersonal. The casket was closed and surrounded by flowers and flags. Nothing about it seemed real. Barry could not help feeling that his father would come back to be with his family.

After the excitement was over, Barry went back to school. His friends told him how sorry they were to hear about his father's death, but they seemed uncomfortable about talking to him. In fact, just about everyone but his friend Ken stayed away from him. Ken stayed close, talking to Barry about the future and the wonderful things that lay ahead. Ken told Barry not to worry; he had the answer to all his problems.

At first, Barry did not understand what Ken meant,

but he felt good when Ken took him to a meeting where everyone made him feel wanted. Barry had never had so much attention before. He welcomed the opportunity of joining the group, even though his mother told him it was a "cult" and he would lose his individuality. After his father died, Barry did not really care about anything, but he felt secure with Ken's group. They would take care of him and teach him a new kind of life. Soon, Barry looked up to the head of the group much as he had looked up to his father. He had a new family, one that would not desert him.

Barry was especially open to the teaching that he received as a new member of the group. Studies show that young people join a new religious group most easily when their parents have just gone through a divorce or when a parent dies. The group tells them they are very important, and the feeling of being chosen is comforting at a time when there has been a loss. For Barry, who had an especially difficult time sorting out his feelings, it was easy to let others help him do his thinking. He could follow the rules and do whatever work was assigned to him as long as he could feel that he belonged. He did not have to dwell on the death of his father and the loss of their future together. He was busy with the work of the group, and the group became his family.

The groups described in this chapter—institutions, foster homes, homosexual partners, street people, and religious communities—all may offer children emotional support similar to that provided by the family, at least in the short term.

7

Feeling Better
About Yourself

How you value yourself plays an important part in what happens to you. No one feels good all the time, but some people have a general feeling of worth that helps them face many kinds of obstacles courageously. They trust themselves and expect to be successful. These expectations color their behavior and they are eager, outgoing, and confident—apt to be winners.

Many people feel they are worthless and see themselves as losers. They do not feel self-assured in any situation, so they are guarded in their actions. This kind of behavior, in which people expect to fail, makes failure more likely. For example, tennis players know that their games are better on days when they feel good about themselves. When there is tension and a feeling of being no good, the chances of losing are greater. This is true in sports and in many everyday situations, too.

People who feel self-confident most of the time do not always feel good about themselves, but Jerry *never* felt good about himself. He insisted that his father would not have left the family if Jerry had not argued with him at his birthday dinner. That was when his father left the table with the remark that he had had enough of the family and went to live with someone else in a nearby town. No matter how hard his mother tried, she could not convince Jerry that his defiance was only a trigger that set something in motion that had been present for a long time. Even before the divorce, Jerry always felt he was worthless. He felt his parents' arguments were all about him, although most of them really were not. The memory of bitter battles made him afraid and held him back from making overtures of friendship to other people. Although he tried a few times, he was positive he would fail, and he did. Jerry spent many sad years feeling sorry for himself because his parents were divorced.

"What can you expect? He comes from a broken home." This kind of remark is usually meant to be unflattering but this may not always be so. Divorce is leaving fewer emotional scars now than it used to. So many of today's children who grow up in homes where parents are separated are facing up to the extra stresses so well, people are taking a new look at the situation.

Almost three thousand children are involved in their parents' divorces every day. Many of these children spend an unusual amount of time questioning their own worth and endure periods that are especially difficult, but in time they show that they can do just as well as those who grow up in intact families, those with the original parents. For children of divorced parents, the divorce, in time, means only a memory of an unhappy year of childhood.

Rather than feeling sorry for themselves, many children of divorce recognize that they are not as lucky as most children who are born to parents who continue to love each other. And there are children whose parents are still living together who are no luckier or happier than children whose parents have separated. In both kinds of families there may be children who do not feel good about themselves and indeed would not in any situation.

What Is Self-esteem?

Feeling good about oneself is known as self-esteem. A person with good self-esteem is not a conceited person, but one who has a quiet sense of self-respect.

"Mary really thinks she is somebody special," says a boy who thinks she is conceited. Actually, Mary is wearing a mask of noisy conceit. Inside, she feels unlovable, but she hides her feelings by appearing self-confident and perfect. She works to appear this way, using her energy to seem confident rather than being so. Still, there are people who recognize that she is just a little too uppity and that her gestures are too exaggerated. They know she is hiding feelings of worthlessness behind this mask of conceit. She is using one of many unhealthy defenses to hide inadequacy.

Psychologists and psychiatrists associate self-esteem and self-confidence with potential for happiness. The person who is trying hard to impress people has less time and energy for more productive activities and recreation. People with low self-esteem restrict their lives because they do not have the courage to risk new experiences.

If your self-esteem is high, you are glad you are you. You do not waste energy trying to impress others because you know you have value. You can use that energy in more valuable ways, knowing that you have something to offer others.

Divorce and Self-esteem

Many things connected with divorce can contribute to lowering a child's self-esteem. For example, most parents who are separating are deeply involved with new burdens. They may give children the feeling that they are an added economic hardship, that they interfere with a career, that they interfere with a parent's future relationships with the opposite sex, and so on. A child may sense this and develop a lowered sense of self-worth. Some children are used as the target for a parent who feels resentment toward a husband or wife. Jennifer was such a case.

Jennifer's father was easily irritated over little mannerisms, such as the way she tossed her hair, because this reminded him of his wife, who had left him for another man. When Jennifer visited her father, he often commented that she was just like her mother. It was hard for Jennifer to accept the fact that her father's hostility was really directed against her mother and not against her. His treatment did not help her to feel good about herself.

If a stepparent or one of your own parents makes hostile remarks about your other parent, try to recognize that you are a constant reminder of a part of life that was unpleasant. When parents are tearing one another down, they do not realize that their children usually feel a deep loyalty for both parents that they are struggling to preserve.

Some children suffer because a parent uses the child as a substitute for a missing husband or wife. Such a child feels anxious because he or she cannot provide advice and comfort that only an adult is equipped to handle. Of course, the child does not realize this, but the result is a lowering of the child's self-esteem.

Many children suffer because the behavior of a missing parent was especially bad. For example, Joe's father was an alcoholic who beat the boy's mother whenever he was drunk. Joe not only suffered from the problems at home, his classmates were no help. They taunted him with remarks about his father. They asked Joe if he was going to be a wife-beater or if he could handle his beer better than his father. Joe felt the stigma to the point of becoming shy and hating himself. Only with long-term professional help was he able to see that he did not contribute in any way to his father's behavior and should not blame himself for it. He was helped to realize that the people who ridiculed him had problems with their own behavior, and it was they who should feel ashamed of themselves. Joe found it difficult to realize that he was just unlucky in having a father who behaved the way he did. This did not make *him* bad, and he would not necessarily grow up to be like his father. Eventually, Joe found that people liked him for himself, in spite of his father's reputation.

Through his many talks with the therapist, Joe learned something about his father that he had not been able to understand. From all he saw and heard, his father seemed like a really bad person. Certainly, his father's behavior was bad. However, Joe learned that his father had grown up in a family that was always putting him down, so he had a very bad opinion of himself. These early experiences convinced Joe's father that he was of little or no worth, for no matter how hard he tried he could not earn his parents' love. Frustrated by his inability to gain any satisfaction, his father began to withdraw from the world at an early age in a self-destructive way. When he was upset, he drank until he no longer felt anxious. By the time Joe was born, his father was addicted to alcohol to the degree that there were chemical changes in his body that made him crave it. He had also learned to release some of his hate by striking out at people who crossed him. Unfortunately, Joe's mother was often the target.

Although Joe's father's problems were very complicated and he would never fully understand them, Joe could at least realize that his father was not a bad man and that Joe himself did not come from "bad stock."

Building Self-esteem

Fortunately, one's self-esteem can change. A person who thinks he or she is worthless can find messages from a variety of people that help in building better self-esteem.

Craig thought he was a real disappointment to his father and his stepmother. He tried to bulldoze his way to acceptance by fighting and acting cool, but he really felt small and worthless inside. His search for a way to count in the eyes of his friends led him to the leadership of a gang that vandalized the school. Vandalizing the school got him prestige and attention from authorities, but it was the wrong kind of attention. Since Craig felt he was no good, he thought he might just as well act that way. But fortunately for Craig, one of his teachers took a special interest in him.

One day, Craig was playing basketball after school, and the coach noticed that he excelled in making baskets. He persuaded Craig to join the school team. Even though Craig did not want to be ridiculed by his gang of friends, he knew he did not really like himself for the trouble he was making. He had to stay at school to sweep the basketball court anyhow as part of his punishment for breaking school windows. Since he had to wait until practice was over, he thought he might as well join the group.

Even though excelling in basketball helped to build Craig's self-esteem, this was not the most important factor in his changed opinion of himself. The coach of the team was trained to help people who were having problems at home and in school. Craig felt he was appreciated by the coach, who encouraged him and praised his strengths rather than dwelling on his bad behavior.

After some success in making new friends, Craig

began to like himself better. He liked himself well enough to know that he did not have to be perfect. When his parents pointed out his shortcomings, he did not give in to them. He had enough positive feelings from other people and other experiences to feel competent and worthwhile.

Perhaps you feel that an unhappy childhood has ruined your life. Not everyone is as fortunate as Craig, but everyone can help himself or herself to feel less worthless.

According to the research of some psychologists, a happy childhood is not the key to adult happiness. Professor Jonathan Freedman of Columbia University conducted a survey that indicated the influence of childhood on happiness is weaker than many people have concluded in the past. Many people whose parents died or were divorced, who were treated coldly, and who led unhappy childhoods, Professor Freedman found, still manage to be very happy as adults. The one factor that carries over from childhood to adulthood is guilt, and with guilt comes a feeling of self-loathing. Therefore, it is especially important for children of divorce to realize that they are not the cause of the divorce and that parents are divorcing each other, not the children.

Self-esteem has been called the key to inner peace and happy living. But suppose you think you are unlovable and not worthwhile. Is it too late to do something about it?

Fortunately, people can raise their self-esteem no matter what their age. The feeling of worth has to be learned, so the feeling of worthlessness can be unlearned. People can grow and change all their lives, so they can learn to feel better about themselves.

One way to begin building self-esteem is to make a self-inventory. How aware are you of your special qualities? Since there is no other person in the world exactly like you, you have some capacities and strengths that are special to you. You can make yourself more aware of them and develop and enjoy them more. Perhaps you think you have no special qualities that make you worthwhile. What about being a good listener? The world needs good listeners, but many people's lives are too cluttered with mental trash to hear what others are saying. Children often complain that their parents never listen to them. This may be true because many people do not know how to listen.

You can begin to be a good listener by listening to two other people talking. Did either one hear the other person's point of view or was each person too busy trying to get his or her own message across? Did either person give concrete evidence that a message was received?

Now try listening to someone in your own family. When someone tells you about certain feelings, reflect about this and then try to understand from that person's point of view. For example, suppose your stepmother tells you that she is tired of driving you and your sister to school, to your friends' houses, to your music lesson, or to other places where you must be taken and picked up. At first, you might think it is her job to drive you or think it isn't your fault she has to do this, but try to consider her point of view. Try responding to her in a way that shows you understand how she feels. If you tell her you can see that all this driving must be a problem for her, she knows you have heard her. You have been a good listener. You are helping her by listening.

Being a good listener, painting, singing, helping others, trying to understand others, playing games for fun but resisting the temptation to manipulate people, and an almost endless number of other things can help you to feel better about yourself. Just knowing you can feel better is a good beginning. Just knowing you are not trapped because your parents have separated or remarried, but are just one of millions of others who have had this kind of bad luck, can help.

Joining a group of people who have had similar family experiences can be extremely helpful. In some communities, teenagers of divorced parents have formed self-help groups in which they sort out feelings and give one another support. Groups may meet weekly under the supervision of a school guidance counselor or a leader from the community. There may be such a group in your area, or you may want to ask an adviser to help you start this kind of a group.

International Youth Council, the program for young people that is sponsored by the organization Parents Without Partners, was mentioned in chapter 3. Remember, anyone can join who is between the ages of twelve and seventeen and whose parents are separated, divorced, widowed, or never married.

Other organizations where you may find companionship and support are listed at the back of the book. Many of the members of these groups come from single-parent homes or live in stepfamilies. Such groups help you to meet others who feel the same way you do. It helps to know that you are not the only one who harbors some bad thoughts and feelings and that you are not alone in trying to cope with important aspects of family life. These groups can help you to develop self-respect.

If you do not treat yourself with respect, you cannot expect others to do so. If you play the game of running yourself down, you can expect this kind of treatment from others. But if you are friendly and loving to yourself, you can do more to nurture others.

Do you tolerate your own mistakes? Remember, you can discard whatever is unfitting and replace it with something better. You are living in the present, and everything about you belongs to you. You can learn to see the glass of water half full along with the optimists rather than half empty along with the pessimists, and to see the good in yourself.

Perhaps you will find it helpful to make a list each evening of the good things that happened to you and the good things you did during the day. Many people who do this find that they like themselves better when they learn to concentrate on the good.

Liking yourself better may be especially hard when you feel that a parent or stepparent dislikes you, but you can be aware that such feelings may be colored by complicated emotions that involve others. Although divorce can be a blow to self-esteem in many ways, the blow need not do permanent damage. You can help it heal.

Where to Get Help

If you cannot find a local group of one of these organizations, write to the national headquarters listed below to find out if there is a branch near you. You will find companionship when you join and a chance to develop new interests. You will probably find many members whose parents have been divorced.

Big Brothers–Big Sisters of America
230 North 13th Street
Philadelphia, PA 19107

Boys Clubs of America
771 First Avenue
New York, NY 10017

Boy Scouts of America
1325 Walnut Hill Lane
Irving, TX 75038

Camp Fire Girls, Inc.
4601 Madison Avenue
Kansas City, MO 64112

Girls Clubs of America
441 West Michigan Street
Indianapolis, IN 46202

National 4-H Council
7100 Connecticut Avenue
Chevy Chase, MD 20815

Parents Without Partners
International Youth Council
7910 Woodmont Avenue NW
Washington, DC 20814

YMCA (Young Men's Christian Association)
101 North Wacker Drive
Chicago, IL 60606

YMHA (Young Men's Hebrew Association)
1395 Lexington Avenue
New York, NY 10128

YWCA (Young Women's Christian Association)
726 Broadway
New York, NY 10003

YWHA (Young Women's Hebrew Association)
1395 Lexington Avenue
New York, NY 10128

For help with special kinds of problems:

If a parent is an **alcoholic,** contact Al-Anon Family Group Headquarters, P.O. Box 862, Midtown Station, New York, NY, to find out if there is a local Alateen group near you. One might be listed in your telephone book if you live in a large city.

If a parent has a **gambling** problem, contact Gam-Anon, P.O. Box 967, Radio City Station, New York, NY 10101.

If someone is **abducted** by a parent who does not have custody, contact National Center for Missing and Exploited Children, 1835 K Street NW, Washington, DC 20006.

If you are a **runaway** and want to let your parents know you are safe, you can call either of the following numbers toll-free without identifying your location to your parents. Operators will help you to find shelter or to get home again if that is what you wish.

National Runaway Switchboard
1-800-621-4000 Nationwide
1-800-972-6004 in Illinois

Runaway Hotline
1-800-231-6946 Nationwide
1-800-392-3352 in Texas

If someone in your family has been or is in **prison** and you want to meet others whose parents have had the same experience, contact the Fortune Society, 39 West 19th Street, New York, NY 10011.

Short-term counseling helps many children of parents who have separated and remarried. In addition to help from school counselors, religious advisers, and medical doctors in general practice, some children are finding support from community and school programs.

If you want **in-depth counseling,** finding the person who can help you most may take some searching. The quality of care varies and each case is different. To find the services that best suit your need, try the following agencies and associations. Most of them are listed in a separate section in the back of your local telephone book.

Child Guidance Center

Community Mental Health Center

Mental Health Association

Family or Youth Services

American Psychiatric Association

American Psychological Association

Choose a therapist whose qualifications are licensed and who has had experience with your type of problem. You and your parents can inquire about qualifications and fees.

Suggested Reading

Anderson, Hal W., and Gail S. Anderson. *Mom and Dad Are Divorced, but I'm Not: Parenting After Divorce.* Chicago: Nelson-Hall, 1981.

Boeckman, Charles. *Surviving Your Parents' Divorce.* New York: Franklin Watts, 1980.

Booher, Dianna Daniels. *Coping When Your Family Falls Apart.* New York: Julian Messner, 1979.

Craven, Linda. *Stepfamilies: New Patterns in Harmony.* New York: Julian Messner, 1982.

Dolmetsch, Paul, and Alexa Shih, eds. *The Kids' Book About Single Parent Families.* Garden City, N.Y.: Doubleday & Co., 1985.

Fayerweather Street School. *The Kids' Book of Divorce: By, For, and About Kids.* Ed. Eric E. Rofes. Lexington, Mass.: Stephen Greene Press, 1981.

Fackre, Linda Bird. *Growing Up Divorced.* New York: Simon & Schuster, 1983; Fawcett Book Group, 1984.

Gay, Kathlyn. *Changing Families: Meeting Today's Challenges.* Hillside, N.J.: Enslow Publishers, 1988.

Getzoff, Ann, and Carolyn McClenahan. *Stepkids: A Survival Guide for Teenagers in Stepfamilies.* New York: Walker & Co., 1984.

Gilbert, Sara D. *Trouble at Home.* New York: Lothrop, Lee & Shepard, 1981.

Hyde, Margaret Oldroyd, and Lawrence E. Hyde. *Missing Children.* New York: Franklin Watts, 1985.

Ives, Sally Blakeslee, David Fassler, and Michele Lash. *The Divorce Workbook: A Guide for Kids and Families.* Burlington, Vt.: Waterfront Books, 1985.

Krementz, Jill. *How It Feels to Be Adopted.* New York: Alfred A. Knopf, 1982.

————. *How It Feels When Parents Divorce.* New York: Alfred A. Knopf, 1984.

LeShan, Eda J. *What's Going to Happen to Me? When Parents Separate or Divorce.* New York: Four Winds Press, 1978; rev. ed., 1986.

Lewis, Helen Coale. *All About Families: The Second Time Around.* Atlanta: Peachtree Publishers, 1980.

Lindsay, Jeanne Warren. *Do I Have a Daddy? A Story About a Single-Parent Child, with a Special Section for Single Mothers and Fathers.* Buena Park, Calif.: Morning Glory Press, 1982.

List, Julie Autumn. *The Day the Loving Stopped: A Daughter's View of Her Parents' Divorce.* New York: Fawcett Book Group, 1981.

Mayle, Peter. *Divorce Can Happen to the Nicest People.* New York: Macmillan Co., 1979.

Powledge, Fred. *So You're Adopted.* New York: Charles Scribner's Sons, 1982.

Richards, Arlene, and Irene Willis. *How to Get It Together When Your Parents Are Coming Apart.* New York: David McKay Co., 1976.

Robson, Bonnie. *My Parents Are Divorced Too: Teenagers Talk About Their Experiences and How They Cope.* New York: Everest House, 1980.

Spilke, Francine Susan. *What About Me? Understanding Your Parents' Divorce.* New York: Crown Publishers, 1979.

Troyer, Warner. *Divorced Kids: Children of Divorce Speak Out and Give Advice to Mothers, Fathers, Lovers, Stepparents, Brothers, Sisters, Boyfriends, Girlfriends, and Each Other.* New York: Harcourt Brace Jovanovich, 1979.

Vigeveno, H. S., and Anne Claire. *No One Gets Divorced Alone.* Ventura, Calif.: Regal Books, 1987.

Index